BLACK TEACHERS
ON
TEACHING

BLACK TEACHERS
ON
TEACHING

Michele Foster

THE NEW PRESS • NEW YORK

LIBRARY OF CONGRESS CATALOGING-IN-PUBLICATION DATA

FOSTER, MICHELE.

BLACK TEACHERS ON TEACHING / MICHELE FOSTER.

P.   CM.

ISBN 1-56584-320-7

1. AFRO-AMERICAN TEACHERS — UNITED STATES — BIOGRAPHY.

2. AFRO-AMERICAN TEACHERS — UNITED STATES — HISTORY. I. TITLE.

LA2311.F67   1997

371.1'0092'2 — DC20   96-9479

[B]   CIP

PUBLISHED IN THE UNITED STATES BY THE NEW PRESS, NEW YORK

DISTRIBUTED BY W. W. NORTON & COMPANY, INC., NEW YORK

ESTABLISHED IN 1990 AS A MAJOR ALTERNATIVE TO THE LARGE COMMERCIAL
PUBLISHING HOUSES, THE NEW PRESS IS A NONPROFIT AMERICAN BOOK PUB-
LISHER. THE PRESS IS OPERATED EDITORIALLY IN THE PUBLIC INTEREST,
RATHER THAN FOR PRIVATE GAIN; IT IS COMMITTED TO PUBLISHING IN INNOVA-
TIVE WAYS WORKS OF EDUCATIONAL, CULTURAL, AND COMMUNITY VALUE THAT,
DESPITE THEIR INTELLECTUAL MERITS, MIGHT NOT NORMALLY BE COMMER-
CIALLY VIABLE. THE NEW PRESS'S EDITORIAL OFFICES ARE LOCATED AT THE CITY
UNIVERSITY OF NEW YORK.

BOOK DESIGN BY ANN ANTOSHAK

PRODUCTION MANAGEMENT BY KIM WAYMER

PRINTED IN THE UNITED STATES OF AMERICA

9 8 7 6 5 4 3 2 1

In memory of my grandparents,
Anna Humphrey Walker and George Walker;
To my mother, Vivienne Foster Erlandson;
and my son, Touré Foster

Contents

Foreword

A few years ago I spoke at a conference about my own education in the segregated South and my very positive experiences with the black teachers and the all-black schools I attended. I ended my statement by saying that we needed to look at the past through new eyes in order to determine what we might learn to help address the apparently difficult educational issue of providing an excellent education for all African-American children. A white progressive educator from New York, who by her own admission had never visited the South, stood up and angrily told me that I was romanticizing the past and doing irreparable harm to all the progress that had been made during the past few decades. After all, she continued, if segregated black schools were so wonderful, then why did black people fight so hard to integrate?

This statement, often repeated in one form or another, is emblematic of a debilitating myth embedded within the struggle for civil rights that continues to haunt African Americans. Namely, that the reason black people fought so hard for desegregation is that deep down they agreed with the larger society's view that without access to white culture, white teachers, white schools, and white leadership, black people could never adequately educate their children, nor hope to create a decent future for their race. Of course, the real reason for the school desegregation struggle was to gain the economic benefits and resources for black children that were commonly provided for white children.

But the truth was little ammunition against the destructive myth. The resulting misguided and racist paternalism was responsible in part for the mass closures of black schools and the mass layoffs of black teachers during the integration process, as discussed in this book. After all, white teachers would make education *so* much better for poor black children stuck in predominantly black schools, and, of course, those fortunate enough to attend previously all-white schools deserved, along with their white classmates, the best —i.e. the whitest — teaching force possible.

Even now the myth lives on with similar consequences. Throughout the nation, state policies are regularly implemented to insure the reduction in numbers of African-American teachers. Georgia, for example, while officially bemoaning the dearth of black teachers, is presently considering a change from a state certification test which eliminated 40 percent of the African-American teacher candidates to one which will eliminate 70 percent. When I was in Baltimore a few years ago, a group of white educational leaders apparently believed that almost *any* white person could do a better job educating black children than the black teachers who then formed the majority in the system. Consequently, policies were implemented to give hiring preference to predominantly white Groups who had not been educated as teachers over African-American candidates who had completed at least four years of teacher education at one of the local historically black colleges or universities. During the course of one year, several projects in that vein were initiated: extensive efforts were made to bring into Baltimore schools white Peace Corps workers who were not trained as teachers, but who had worked in African and other "Third World" village schools; college students who were not preparing to be educators but who thought they might like to try teaching for one or two years were heavily recruited to work in the predominantly black school district; and, after the young white assistant to a state politician was turned down for a teaching job in Baltimore because he was not certified (he had an undergraduate degree in history from Harvard), liberal alternative certification procedures were adopted at the state level to allow college graduates from any discipline to become teachers with little preparation in the teaching profession.

Despite numerous thinly veiled efforts to reduce the numbers of black teachers, those of us — black and white — who have worked closely with African-American teachers know that many of them have provided magical classrooms for poor, African-American children. I once interviewed Mrs. Amanda Grace, a retired teacher who started her career in one-room schools in rural Louisiana. "Miss Amanda," as she was known to her students, regularly taught enough content and love-of-learning by the end of third grade (when many children had to drop out to take on various family responsibilities) to allow her students to pass entrance tests for civil service jobs as adults. My own mother, as a teacher in segregated Louisiana, told of a white supervisor who regularly visited black teachers' classrooms in order to get ideas for inservice courses for white teachers. Vanessa Siddle Walker, in her book, *Their Highest Potential*, describes a school and its teachers in segregated North Carolina which provided an excellent education for its poor, black clientele. And of course, scholars like Gloria Ladson-Billings and Annette Henry have chronicled the stories of present-day teachers who are continuing to break the back of the pernicious myth.

Yet, we have not before had in one volume — and in their own voices — the perspectives, values, and pedagogical insights of a group of excellent African-American teachers from diverse communities across our nation. The teachers represented here include those who have already retired from the classroom, veteran teachers still practicing, and novice teachers who are struggling with the difficult circumstances facing their students and themselves in urban school systems.

But these teachers do have commonalities. Teachers like them have been described as being "culturally relevant" (Gloria Ladson-Billings' *The Dreamkeepers*) and engaged in "emancipatory pedagogies" (Joyce King in Michele Foster's previous work, *Qualitative Investigations into Schools and Schooling*). In other words, these teachers are committed to African-American children and the communities which spawn them: to believing in their unlimited potential, to working hard to provide a quality education despite difficult circumstances, to struggling against (and helping their students struggle against) all forms of racial oppression, and to building a sense of connection between students and their communities.

By including a multi-age cohort, Foster does a great service. It becomes obvious that the pernicious myth is not only false, but has been so for many, many years. Perhaps we can finally set the record straight. While all teachers are invited and welcome in the struggle to educate all black children, there is so much that white and black teachers and teacher educators can learn from the teachers whose voices we hear in this book — these exceptional, dedicated, and committed African-American teachers who invested and continue to invest their all into educating the African-American— indeed, the American— future.

LISA D. DELPIT
Benjamin E. Mays Professor of
Urban Educational Leadership
Georgia State University

Acknowledgments

There are many people who have helped make this book a reality. I want to acknowledge the support of colleagues, friends, and students at the various institutions where I have hung my hat since I began this project in 1988. Thanks to Michelle Fine and Vivian Gadsden, who supported me while I was at the University of Pennsylvania. The generosity and camaraderie of Susan Knight and Pam DeGraffenreid made my postdoctoral fellowship at the University of North Carolina more fulfilling that it would otherwise have been. I applaud Jeffrey Lewis and Jeanne Russell, graduate students at the University of California, Davis, for their spunk, spirit, and determination not to compromise themselves or to be dominated.

I am indebted to my research assistants Jeanne Newman at the University of Pennsylvania, who transcribed many of the first interviews, and Tryphenia Peele at The Claremont Graduate School, who did the research and prepared the tables and whose assistance during the past two years has been invaluable.

Thanks to Teresa Wilborn, who on short notice retyped part of the manuscript that was lost when my computer was stolen.

I acknowledge the financial support of the University of Pennsylvania Research Foundation, the Spencer Small Grants Program, The National Academy of Education Spencer Postdoctoral Fellowship Program, The Carolina Minority Postdoctoral Program, The Smithsonian Faculty Fellowship Program, and The National Endowment of Humanities Summer Seminar for College Teachers.

I wish to express my gratitude to Dawn Davis, who believed in the project from the beginning and who had faith that the book would be completed even when I had given up hope. Her editorial comments have greatly improved this book.

Special thanks to Michael Yeong for his patience, encouragement, and humor.

Finally, I am especially indebted to the teachers who opened up their classrooms, homes, and lives to my inquiry. Although all those mentioned have made this book possible, I alone am responsible for any of its shortcomings.

Introduction

During the summer of 1994, while browsing in the public library in Lawrence, Kansas, I read the following item in the 10–16 June 1994 issue of *The Call*, a Kansas City weekly black newspaper established in 1919:

> Mrs. Mary Ella Tymony, 99, formerly a teacher in Moberly, Mo., and in Kansas City died Sunday, June 5, at the Timberlake Nursing Care Center where she had been a patient for the last seven years. Mrs. Tymony was widely known in this area for her work in education and in civil rights. Mrs. Tymony was born in Huntsville, Mo., one of the seven children of the late Charley and Martha Smith Hicks. She lived in the Kansas City area over 50 years. She was a member of the Paseo Baptist Church and its Women's Missionary Union. She was a graduate of Lincoln University, Jefferson City, Mo. She received her Master's of Education Degree in Guidance from the University of Missouri at Columbia. She was the former Dean of Students at Lincoln University, she [sic] was a member of the National Education Association, the Missouri State Teachers Association, former member in Moberly, Mo., an active member of the NAACP and served as the Missouri State Conference Branch Treasurer for eight years. She was an educator with the Kansas City Missouri School District before retiring. Her final years of teaching were at the Western Baptist Bible College. She leaves Bernard C. DeCoteau of the Center; one stepdaughter, Audrey Wynn of Miami, Fla.; two nieces, Nellie Mae Tolson of Moberly Mo., Helen D. Collins of Rock Island, Ill., and other relatives.[1]

Except to friends and relatives, this obituary was probably of little interest. Although I was not personally acquainted with

---

[1] *The Call* (10–16 June 1994), pp 2, 15–16.

the woman whose life it memorialized, my eyes fastened on it. Having interviewed black teachers for a life history project, I had seen her name in archival sources.

Mary Ella Tymony taught in Moberly, a small northeast Missouri town approximately sixty-five miles from Jefferson City (the state capital) and twenty-five miles from Columbia (the site of the flagship campus of the University of Missouri). In 1959, five years after the *Brown vs. Board of Education* decision, she was one of eight plaintiffs in the *Naomi Brooks et al. v. School District of the City of Moberly Missouri*, where all eleven black teachers had been dismissed.[2] There was much publicity around the case. In May 1956 the *Southern School News* reported the "facts." In November of the same year, the paper revisited the case in an article discussing the displacement of black teachers resulting from desegregation.[3] Having followed the newspaper accounts, I knew that none of the eleven teachers had been reinstated in Moberly. Mrs. Tymony eventually secured a position at the historically black Lincoln University in Jefferson City. The obituary made me wonder what more there was to her story beyond the facts of the lawsuit and what was reported in the newspaper.

At the age of ninety-nine, however, Mrs. Tymony died with her story. But her obituary inspired me to complete my oral history project, during the course of which I have discovered the stories of many previously unknown black teachers like Mary Ella Tymony. Despite their exclusion from history books, they are part of the long line of teachers who have taught black children for two hundred years.

In a lecture delivered at Harvard University in 1950, Margaret Mead noted that "Teachers who are members of any group who are in a minority in their particular community will have to add

---

[2] *Naomi Brooks et al. v. School District of City of Moberly, Missouri etc., et al.*, United States Court of Appeals, Eighth Circuit (June 17, 1959), 267F.2d 733, in *Race Relations Law Reporter*, vol. 4, pp. 613–618.

[3] "Missouri's Teacher Tenure Hearings Expected to Develop 'Case History,'" *Southern School News* 2 (May 1956), p.8; "462 Negro Teachers Out, Many Land in New Jobs," *Southern School News* 3, no. 5 (November 1956), pp. 1–2.

in their own words that they are Negro teachers . . . as the case may be, redefining themselves against an image of woman who for most of the country is white, middle-class, middle-aged, and of Protestant background."[4] This comment, delivered forty-seven years ago, succinctly captures the condition of black teachers today, whose numbers are in sharp decline. Mead's commentary also describes the treatment of black teachers in scholarly literature where they are not well represented. This is true even though during the three decades following emancipation and the first six decades of the twentieth century teaching, along with the ministry, was one of the few occupations open to college-educated blacks. "The only thing an educated Negro can do is teach or preach," people would say. One difference between teaching and preaching, of course, was that teaching was open to women on an equal basis. In fact, one of the primary leadership roles available to black women was as teachers in their communities. Throughout history black teachers were more likely to be employed in states where there were larger numbers of black pupils and where schools were segregated.

Census data from the middle of the nineteenth century through the early twentieth century illustrate these patterns. Between 1890 and 1910 the number of blacks who were employed as teachers rose from 15,100 to 66,236. In the census years of 1890, 1900, and 1910, black teachers represented about 44, 45, and 45 percent, respectively, of professional blacks. In 1910, 76 percent of black teachers employed were women. The 1850 census compares the number of black teachers in two cities and two states, Northern and Southern. In that year, there were fifteen black and mulatto teachers in Louisiana but none in Connecticut. In that same year in New York there were eight black and mulatto teachers and twelve in New Orleans.[5]

The importance to the black community of teaching as a profession can be seen in reference material and other literature

---

[4] Margaret Mead, *The School in American Culture* (Cambridge, Mass.: Harvard University Press, 1950).
[5] *Negro Population in the United States, 1790–1915* (New York: Arno Press, 1968), p.511.

about blacks. For example, of the 641 biographies of individual black women contained in the two-volume reference work *Black Women in America: An Historical Encyclopedia*, edited by Darlene Clark Hine, 113 entries (18 percent) are indexed under the term "educator." A close reading of this encyclopedia reveals a larger number of individuals who, though not classified as educators, were temporarily employed as teachers. Another encyclopedia, *Notable Black American Women*, lists 150 educators among its entries.[6] Also included among the listings in *The Dictionary of American Negro Biography* are numerous biographies of both male and female teachers.[7] Seventy-four of the 450 entries (16 percent) contained in a bibliography of black American autobiographies written through 1974 list teaching as a profession or occupation.[8] More than a dozen of the women interviewed as part of the black women's oral history project archived at Radcliffe University served as teachers at one time in their lives. Included among the forty-seven older Southern black women profiled in the book *Hope and Dignity* are seventeen teachers. Finally, material on black teachers is embedded in memoirs, studies of black education, and life history studies.[9]

---

[6] Jessie Carney Smith, ed., *Notable Black American Women* (Detroit: Gale Press, 1992).

[7] Rayford W. Logan & Michael R. Winston, comps. *Dictionary of American Negro Biography* (New York: W. W. Norton, 1982).

[8] Russell Brigano, *Black Americans in Autobiography* (Durham: Duke University Press, 1974).

[9] Some of the books or articles in which black teachers have been portrayed include: Houston Baker, "What Charles Knew," in *An Apple for My Teacher: 12 Authors Tell about Teachers who Made the Difference*, ed. L. Rubin Jr. (Chapel Hill: Algonquin Books, 1987); Bob Blauner, *Black Lives, White Lives: Three Decades of Race Relations in America* (Berkeley: University of California Press, 1989); J. L. Chestnut and Julia Cass, *Black in Selma: The Uncommon Life of J. L. Chestnut, Jr.* (New York: Farrar, Straus, and Giroux, 1990); Patricia Hill Collins, *Black Feminist Thought: Knowledge, Consciousness and the Politics of Empowerment* (Boston: Unwin Hyman, 1990); Evelyn Fairbanks, *Days of Rondo* (St. Paul: Minnesota Historical Society Press, 1990); Mamie Fields with Karen Fields, *Lemon Swamp: A Carolina Memoir* (New York: The Free Press, 1985); Walt Harrington, *Crossings: A White Man's Journey into Black America* (New York: Harper Collins, 1992); belle

Despite these long years of service by black teachers to the black community, there was never a book—until this one—devoted entirely to a narrative rendering of their experiences. This book is about some of these teachers. Readers will hear the voices of twenty black teachers born between 1905 and 1973. This volume is part of the growing scholarship that examines the experiences of blacks who have been employed in substantial numbers or exclusively in occupations such as the Pullman porters, the nursing profession, or the postal service, and highlighted in such works as *Miles of Smiles* and *Black Women in White*.[10] Given the significance of teaching as a profession within the black community and the growing scholarship examining occupations that have typically employed large numbers of blacks, the absence of a book devoted to black teachers is both puzzling and disturbing.

This book is also part of a trend that reflects a growing movement among social historians to record the experiences of blacks who until the civil rights movement were compelled by force of law to live as second-class citizens. A project at Duke University entitled "Behind the Veil: African-American Life in the Jim Crow Era" is documenting the lives and experiences of blacks who lived in the South between the end of the Civil War and the civil rights period. A collaborative project between Wayne State University and a consortium of historically black colleges will document the work of ninety-five historically black colleges. It will assemble all the published and unpublished, written and oral material available on their struggles to educate blacks in the United States.

---

hooks, *Talking Back: Thinking Feminist, Thinking Black* (Boston: South End Press, 1989); Clara B. Kennan, "The First Negro Teacher in Little Rock," *Black Women in United States History,* ed. Darlene Clark Hine (Brooklyn: Carlson Publishing, 1990), pp. 773–783; Richard Kluger, *Simple Justice* (New York: Vintage, 1975); Sara Lawrence Lightfoot, *Balm in Gilead: Journey of a Healer* (Reading, Mass.: Addison-Wesley, 1988).

[10] Jack Santino, *Miles of Smiles, Years of Struggle: Stories of Black Pullman Porters* (Urbana: University of Illinois, 1989); Darlene Clark Hine, *Black Women in White: Racial Conflict and Cooperation in the Nursing Profession, 1890–1950* (Bloomington: Indiana University Press, 1989).

Like the large-scale projects underway at Duke and Wayne State University, *Black Teachers on Teaching* strives to understand both the objective and subjective experiences of black teachers.

Methodologically, this book is similar to *My Soul Is My Own; Drylongso: A Self-Portrait of Black America; Black Lives, White Lives;* and *Hope and Dignity* in that it allows the narrators to speak in their own words.[11] Utilizing a life history approach to collecting the experiences of black teachers, this book is an effort to explore and document the constraints and supports in their professional lives and to examine how their experiences have changed over their careers and over the years.

In short, this book seeks to understand how teaching has been experienced and understood by blacks engaged in the profession. The book is comprised of twenty life history interviews that I conducted with black teachers between 1988 and 1996.

I located these teachers through a process I developed and call "community nomination."[12] The interviews were recorded in the teachers' homes and workplaces. The first section provides an historical background to some of the themes that surfaced in the interviews.

The life history method employed in this book is particularly appropriate for several reasons. Life history and the associated techniques of oral history and personal narratives are forms of analysis that can bring the experiences of blacks, including

---

[11] Gwendolyn Etter-Lewis, *My Soul Is My Own: Oral Narratives of African-American Women in the Professions* (New York: Routledge, 1993); John Langston Gwaltney, *Drylongso: A Self-Portrait of Black America* (New York: Random House, 1980); Blauner, *Black Lives, White Lives: Three Decades of Race Relations in America,* (Berkeley: University of California Press, 1989); Herring Wilson and Susan Mullally, *Hope and Dignity: Older Black Women of the South* (Philadelphia: Temple University Press, 1983).

[12] "Community nomination," a term coined specifically for this project, is a selection process I developed in which the names of teachers were solicited through direct contact with individual black communities. Others have used similar processes. In *Daddy's Gone to War: The Second World War and America's Children* (New York: Oxford University Press, 1993), William Tuttle uses community appeal to solicit narratives of the memories of individuals whose fathers served in the front during World War II.

teachers, into view in ways that reveal the complexity of their experiences. Life history not only provides material about individual lives but also offers the opportunity to explore how individual lives are shaped by society. Thus life history research offers critical insights into larger social processes by connecting the lives of individuals to society. First-person accounts have long been employed by individuals to encode and record the experiences of blacks, and such accounts have served as a valuable source of information for both scholars seeking to understand the black community and for the black community itself.

Although I did not have a fixed set of questions to ask, I did have a set of topics that I covered in all the interviews. The topics included the social, economic, and cultural milieu of the teachers' families and communities; their schooling and teaching experiences; their friends, mentors, and other influences on their lives; their reasons for choosing a career in teaching; their philosophies of teaching; their perceptions of students; their understanding of teachers' roles; and the changes they have observed over the course of their careers.

The process of conducting life history research and the political and ethical dilemmas that arise when interpreting life histories are the subject of intense debate. One of the central issues in this debate is whether outsiders or insiders (individuals from the same cultural and speech communities) are better suited to conducting research in communities of color. While belonging to the same speech and cultural community as one's narrators can facilitate the recovery of authentic accounts, even interviewers and narrators who share social and cultural characteristics are likely to be separated by other important characteristics.

Like my narrators, I am black and have been a teacher for many years. But I was separated from a number of my narrators in other equally important ways. I am a young woman from the urban North who interviewed men, Southerners, rural residents, and older teachers. Despite these differences, my interactions with my narrators were generally positive, marked by empathy and trust, and mirrored those reported by Gwaltney, a black anthropologist who conducted a major study of blacks in the 1970s. For instance, the teachers often invited me to participate in their daily activities; I accompanied some of them to church and other community meetings, ate dinner with their friends and families, and at their insistence sometimes spent the night in their homes instead of a hotel. I often reciprocated by assisting them in their classrooms, by talking with their students, and in some rare cases by developing more substantial relationships with their students through correspondence.

My interest in this topic was nurtured long ago while I was growing up with my mother and maternal grandparents in a house built by my great-great-grandfather, a runaway bondsman. He fled slavery in 1857, eventually settling and building a house in Marlborough, Massachusetts, in 1870. He and his wife, Annie Brown Goins, raised eleven children, one of whom, Geneva Goins Young, was my maternal great-grandmother.

I was raised on my family's stories: the story of my great-uncles who moved to Bermuda, married Bermudian women, opened a music shop in the islands, and according to family legend first introduced the snare drum to the island. Throughout my childhood I heard the stories of the more immediate members of my family: my grandfather, a Pullman porter and a founding member of the Brotherhood of Sleeping Car Porters; my grandmother, a showgirl in the black Broadway musicals during the 1920s; my mother, who attended Harlem School of Nursing during the 1940s. Although I reveled in these stories because they linked me to a proud family, I was not aware of their significance until much later in life. I discovered that my grandfather and grandmother had been actors in the panorama of the long history of black Americans. I was even more surprised when my cousin came across the September 1902 issue of *The Colored American Magazine* and found a story about the musical career of Mrs. Ida Goins Wilson, my great-aunt. When my grandmother and I discussed the magazine, she pointed to the picture of Mrs. Marshall Walter Taylor on the cover, telling me that they had been good friends. Major Taylor was once the fastest bicyclist in the world.[13] Initially, I was amazed

---

[13] *The Colored American Magazine* (Boston: The Colored Co-operative Publishing Company, September, 1902), pp. 344, 374.

to learn that my forebears themselves were tucked into the historical record and that they were familiar with other blacks who were part of history. But as this research proceeded I came to realize that this was also true in my case. For instance, while poring over the archives at Hampton University, I found that three people whom I knew from Camp Atwater[14] were graduates of the class of 1968. I also determined that the daughter of a family acquaintance had graduated that same year and that the former spouse of a teacher colleague from the 1970s had been a junior at Hampton that same year. Finally, I recognized the names of three people—two faculty members and one student—whom I have subsequently come to know through my work in academia.

The teachers whose narratives are contained in this book exemplify some of the class, age, and geographic diversity within the black community. Although only five of the twenty narrators are men, this approximates the percentage of black male teachers listed in the 1990 census. According to that census, of 439,176 black teachers, only 91,026 (21 percent) were male. About half of the teachers interviewed grew up in communities segregated by law, while the others spent their childhood in areas where no laws enforced segregation. Eleven of the teachers grew up in urban communities; the remainder grew up in rural communities or in small towns of under 10,000 residents. The teachers were born between 1905 and 1973, and their teaching experience ranged from three to sixty-eight years. Half the teachers have been employed primarily in elementary school; the remainder (all of the men except one), in middle, junior, or senior high schools.

---

[14] Located in East Brookfield, Massachusetts, in 1920, Camp Atwater was willed to the Springfield Urban League. In its early years it was the only major U.S. camp owned and operated by blacks. During the years that segregation prohibited blacks from attending many camps in the United States, black children from all over the country were sent to Camp Atwater. Some of the Atwater's most famous campers include Coleman Young, former mayor of Detroit; Daniel "Chappie" James, a five-star general in the United States Air Force; Clifford Alexander, former Secretary of the Army. Forced to close in 1973, in part a victim of desegregation, Camp Atwater reopened its doors in 1980.

Although some of the teachers were serving as administrators or were retired at the time of interview, most had spent many years employed as teachers, most having begun when segregated schools were the norm. Consequently, most of these teachers have taught in schools populated by large numbers of black students. Thirteen of the teachers have been employed in cities: four taught in the same community in which they were raised. Collectively, these teachers have been employed in twenty-one school districts.[15]

BLACK TEACHERS IN HISTORICAL CONTEXT

Prior to emancipation, blacks held in slavery were forbidden to learn to read. Despite these prohibitions and severe punishments, blacks valued literacy and many learned to read despite these restrictions.[16] Some were taught by sympathetic whites; others learned alongside their master's children. But a significant number were taught by free blacks or by slaves who were literate themselves. Well regarded and respected, these black teachers understood both the power and danger associated with literacy. Leroy Lovelace, a retired high school English teacher, underscores the power of education: "When a people can think critically, they can change things. They are less likely to be taken advantage of and more likely to be able to avoid the traps that others set for us. An uneducated people can be taken advantage of because of their ignorance or naiveté."

---

[15] The teachers are or have been employed in San Diego, Boston, Baltimore, Cleveland, Los Angeles, Riverside County (California), Hartford, Orlando, Philadelphia, New York City, Chicago, Washington, D.C., Wheeling (West Virginia), St. Louis, Jacksonville, Charleston, Flint, Berkeley, Lindale (Texas), Pawley's Island (South Carolina), and Pittsboro (North Carolina).

[16] For a discussion on the value and appreciation of literacy, see Frederick Douglass, *Narrative of the Life of Fredrick Douglass, An American Slave, Written by Himself,* ed. Benjamin Quarles (Cambridge: Belknap Press, 1960). Other accounts of the desire for literacy can be found in numerous slave narratives; for examples see Thomas L. Webber, *Deep Like the Rivers: Education in the Slave Quarter Community, 1831–1865* (New York: Norton, 1978), pp. 131–138.

Leonard Collins, a young teacher, is even more adamant: "I want kids to examine their world critically, to question everything. As kids get older they automatically accept the American ideology. But I don't want kids to just be the future; I want them to change the future."

Quoting James Baldwin, Edouard Plummer, a New York junior high school teacher who has taught since the early sixties declares: "Teaching black children is a revolutionary act."

Throughout history, black teachers have been hired primarily to teach black students. Because larger numbers of blacks resided in the South, a policy of "separate but equal" schooling and Southern laws mandating that black teachers could teach only in segregated schools, greater numbers of black teachers were employed in the seventeen Southern and border states. Of the 63,697 black teachers in the United States in 1940, 46,381 were employed in the south.

Northern communities did not have laws segregating black teachers in black schools. As more blacks migrated to Northern cities, the school systems adopted policies that resulted in the de facto segregation of black pupils and teachers. In cities such as Philadelphia, Boston, New York, and Chicago it was customary to assign black teachers to predominantly black schools or to restrict them to particular grades (usually elementary). In Philadelphia the practice of assigning black teachers to all-black schools began in the early twentieth century. It was done, according to the superintendent of schools, "in order to give employment to a group of deserving numbers of the colored race, who by industry and capacity have won their certificates to teach in the public schools of the city." Whatever the reason, as their numbers increased, black teachers and black pupils became segregated in predominantly black schools. Maintaining two separate eligibility lists, one for black teachers and one for white teachers, was one method the school board used to create and maintain all-black schools. Between 1932 and 1948 the number of black teachers doubled, but the pattern of segregation was firmly established. Of 186 elementary schools, ten were all-black. Not until 1935 was the first black teacher appointed to a junior high school, and not until 1947 was the first black teacher assigned to a high school.

In May 1950, in response to charges of bias in hiring patterns, the president of the Philadelphia School Board proclaimed that the public schools were not discriminating against black teachers, because in making assignments the district considered the sentiments of the community. He announced that any efforts to assign black teachers to predominantly white schools would be undertaken carefully and slowly.

In Chicago the unprecedented growth of the black population through migration and deteriorating race relations culminated in the July 1919 Chicago Race Riot. The residential segregation patterns combined to create the conditions for the de facto segregation that came to characterize the Chicago public schools. In 1916, 91.3 percent of all black students attended integrated schools. Four years later, 40 percent of all black students attended segregated schools. By 1930, the number had risen to 82.4 percent. Changes in the staffing patterns of black teachers mirrored the enrollment patterns of black students. In 1917, 41 of approximately 8,000 teachers were black; in 1930, 308 of 13,000 teachers were black. In 1917, three-fifths of Chicago's black teachers worked in integrated schools; by 1930, less than one-third did.

In the 1930s black teachers were three times more likely to be working as substitutes than as permanent teachers, and although they constituted 3.5 percent of all elementary school teachers, black teachers made up less than .9 percent of the secondary school teachers.

As in Philadelphia the policies of the Chicago School Board, as well as the informal policies at the building level, reinforced the segregation of black teachers. Throughout the 1920s and 1930s the Chicago School Board assigned more black teachers to substitute positions rather than to regular positions, no longer appointed black teachers to mixed schools, and ceased advocating for black teachers who met with resistance from white pupils and parents. At the school level, principals had the final word on hiring, could request particular candidates, and could reject those sent by the board. According to a race relations report issued in the mid-1940s, the result was that approximately 90 percent of non-white teachers were teaching in schools whose student population was more than 95 percent black.

In Northern cities, unlike in most of the South, black teachers did not enjoy unrestricted job opportunities within the de facto segregated system. In twenty-six all-black schools in Chicago in 1930, only 34 percent of the faculty was black. In Philadelphia in the mid-1940s, thirty schools with student populations of at least 75 percent black had predominantly white faculties and 140 had not one black teacher. Thus the patterns of teacher employment that emerged in Chicago resembled those in Philadelphia. Black teachers were restricted to segregated black schools and rarely taught white students, but white teachers could teach black and white pupils. As the decade of the 1940s came to a close, the pattern of de facto segregation with black teachers clustered in predominantly black schools was firmly entrenched in Philadelphia, Chicago, New York, and other cities having large black student populations.

As the relationship between employing black teachers and creating more segregated schools tightened, it caught the attention of W. E. B. Du Bois. In a 1920s article entitled "The Tragedy of Jim Crow," in *Crisis*, he described the dilemma of having to attack segregated public schools while at the same time trying to honor and appreciate black teachers. Almost twenty years later, in an article entitled "Winds of Change," in the *Chicago Defender*, DuBois revisited this problem.[17]

This practice of assigning black teachers to predominantly black schools was firmly entrenched when Joelle Vanderall began teaching in Boston in 1952: "At the time I started teaching in Boston most black teachers were assigned to a narrow geographic strip from the South End into Roxbury, between Tremont Street and Washington. Those assigned to schools outside that area had a very hard time."

When Bobbie Duvon, a teacher in West Virginia, first applied to teach in Hartford, Connecticut, in the late 1940s she was

---

[17] W. E. B. Du Bois, "Winds of Change," *Chicago Defender* (13 October 1944), p. 13.

unable to get a permanent position, so each fall she returned to West Virginia. She relocated to Hartford in the early 1950s but was only able to substitute in the public schools. According to census data, no black teachers were employed in Connecticut in 1950. When a principal of the school where Bobbie had been substituting told her to file an application for employment with the school board, Bobbie replied that she already had: ". . . We all knew where that application had gone: it went in the wastebasket because of the color of my skin. This was in fifty-three when there weren't many black teachers in the city."

When I began teaching in the Boston public schools in the late 1960s I encountered the same problem. As a first-year teacher I was assigned only to substitute teach in predominantly black schools and when I finally did secure my own classroom I was assigned as a "provisional" or temporary teacher in predominantly black schools. It wasn't until 1974, the year Boston public schools were desegregated by court order, that I was offered a permanent teaching position.[18]

The primary reason that black teachers were prohibited from teaching white children was the widespread belief firmly entrenched since the nineteenth century that, like others of their race, black teachers were inferior to whites and not suitable to teach white pupils.

In both the North and the South, however, whites retained the prerogative to teach in black schools. In 1911, when Ruby

---

[18] In 1963 thirteen schools in Boston were at least 90 percent black. Two years later the number of predominantly black schools had increased. A study conducted by the Massachusetts State Department of Education found that half of the black students (10,400) attended twenty-eight schools that were at least 80 percent black. Sixteen schools located in the black community were over 96 percent black. Six years later in 1971, 62 percent of the black students attended schools that were at least 70 percent black while 84 percent of the white students attended schools that were at least 80 percent white. Between 1965 and 1971 the number of schools that had more than 50 percent black student enrollment rose from forty-six to sixty-seven. See J. Anthony Lukas, *Common Ground: A Turbulent Decade in the Lives of Three American Families* (New York: Knopf, 1985), pp.126, 130, 132, 216.

Middleton Forsythe began school in Charleston, South Carolina, black teachers were not allowed to teach in the Charleston city schools. Miss Ruby recounts why her mother decided to send her to a private school run by a black teacher: "She said that with all the teachers being white in the public schools, they treated you just plain mean like in slavery days. I was a bit obstinate, and she knew that these white teachers weren't gonna be able to tell me, 'You do so and so, you got to do so and so,' and I would just do it. She thought that having white teachers treat black children like that was too much like slavery." It was not until 1917, after Septima Clark organized black students at Avery Normal School to go door to door in the black community collecting signatures on a petition, that black teachers were able to teach in the city of Charleston.

In the 1940s black teachers in the North were already segregated by custom; black teachers in the South, by law. But in West Coast cities, such as Portland, Sacramento, and Seattle, black teachers were appointed to teach in the public schools for the first time. Only in Los Angeles had black teachers been working prior to the early 1940s. When Josephine Cole, for example, was hired in San Francisco in 1944, she was the first black teacher hired since the 1870s, when black teachers had been needed to staff the Jim Crow schools. Except for a few black women who had tutored black children in their homes between 1900 and 1920, black teachers had difficulty obtaining employment in predominantly white school districts on the West Coast.[19]

Ethel Tanner, a successful principal in San Mateo, tells what happened when she was first hired in the district: "This was a lily-white town in 1960; they didn't have any black teachers. The school board didn't want to hire me, but there was a principal that wanted to. After battling the school board, he did. The summer before school started I was away visiting my brother. When I returned, my husband told me that there had been a lot of com-

---

[19] Albert S. Brossard, *Black San Francisco: The Struggle for Racial Equality in the West, 1900–1954* (Lawrence: University of Kansas, 1993), pp. 43, 280; "School Teachers: Many Cities Appoint Negro Instructors for the First Time to Meet Schoolmarm Shortage," *Ebony* (September 1948), pp. 36–40.

motion over my hiring. People had called my house and yelled, 'Nigger, nigger, nigger,' over the telephone. A group held a community meeting in a local church to protest my hiring. Over several days, I learned what had gone on during my absence. The more I thought about it, the more I decided that I had a right to that job and I wasn't going to let a bunch of racists keep me from it."

Often, as was the case with the Pennsylvania Association of Teachers of Colored Children, black teachers promoted their own employment cause by arguing that many black children were being harmed in mixed schools populated by white teachers, principals, and students. These black teachers also claimed that separate black schools assisted in the development of racial pride. Some members of the black community, especially those who favored integration, condemned black teachers for their self-serving stance.

The black community agreed about the importance of schooling for their children. Far from being of one mind over the means by which to secure the best educational opportunities, the black community has been deeply divided over whether integrated or segregated schools would achieve the best outcome. This was especially true because integrated schools often meant the loss of jobs for black teachers. Black communities across the United States have grappled with this dilemma since the early nineteenth century.[20] Black leaders often weighed in on both sides of the issue. Some believed that by insisting on black teachers the community was acquiescing to segregation. But there was still considerable sentiment within the black community for retain-

---

[20] Michael W. Homel, *Down from Equality: Black Chicagoans and the Public Schools, 1920–41* (Urbana: University of Illinois Press, 1984), p.2; James O. Horton and Lois E. Horton, *Black Bostonians: Family Life and Community Struggle in the Antebellum North* (New York: Holmes and Meier, 1979), pp. 70–76; David Tyack, *The One Best System: A History of American Urban Education* (Cambridge: Harvard University Press, 1974), pp. 112–13; "Segregated Education: Two Views, 1850," in *A Documentary History of the Negro People in the United States*, vol. I, ed. Herbert Aptheker (1951; reprint, New York: Carol Publishing Group, 1990), pp. 297–99.

ing black teachers to teach in black schools.[21] Even though the hiring of black teachers resulted in strengthening the system of segregated schools, blacks fought for teachers of their own race. And many newspaper editors, educators, preachers, and other influential blacks publicly appealed for black teachers to staff black schools. According to an Albany black Baptist preacher, they followed the motto: "Colored schools, colored teachers; colored churches, colored preachers."[22]

Twenty-two years after the historic *Brown v. Board of Education* decision, which outlawed separate but equal schools, local school boards in Minneapolis, Indianapolis, Louisville, and Pittsburgh have requested an end to desegregation plans. Federal courts have already set aside court orders that require desegregation in St. Louis, Wilmington, and Kansas City. Some blacks are also questioning whether the gains of desegregation outweigh the liabilities. Attorney Ted Shaw, legal counsel for the NAACP Legal Defense Fund, has stated: "My sense is a lot of people are saying, 'We're tired of chasing white folks. It's not worth the price we have to pay.' "[23]

Perhaps it was W. E. B. Du Bois, a pragmatist, who although he remained steadfastly committed to a desegregated society throughout his lifetime, best summarized the situation.

> and I know that race prejudice in the United States today is such that most Negroes cannot receive proper education in white institutions. . . . If the public schools of Atlanta, Nashville, New Orleans, and Jacksonville were thrown open to all races today, the education that colored children would get in them would be worse

---

[21] Horton and Horton, *Black Bostonians*; "Segregated Education," ed. Herbert Aptheker; James D. Curry, *The Free Black in American, 1800–1850: The Shadow of the Dream* (Chicago: University of Chicago Press, 1981), p. 169; Howard N. Rabinowitz, "Half a Loaf: The Shift from White to Black Teachers in the Negro Schools of the Urban South, 1865–1890, *Journal of Southern History*, 40, no. 44 (November 1974), pp. 578–79; Carlton Mabee, *Black Education in New York State: From Colonial to Modern Times* (Syracuse: Syracuse University Press).

[22] Mabee, *Black Education in New York State*, p. 99.

[23] James S. Kunen, "The End of Integration" *Time* (29 April 1996) pp. 43, 45.

than pitiable. And in the same way, there are many public school systems in the North where Negroes are admitted and tolerated, but they are not educated; they are crucified. To sum up this: theoretically, the Negro needs neither separate nor mixed schools. What he needs is Education. What he must remember is that there is no magic either in mixed schools or segregated schools. A mixed school with poor unsympathetic teachers, with hostile public opinion, and no teaching of the truth concerning black folk is bad. A segregated school with ignorant placeholders, inadequate equipment, and poor salaries is equally bad. Other things being equal, the mixed school is the broader, more natural basis for the education of all youth. It gives wider contacts; it inspires greater self-confidence; and suppresses the inferiority complex. But other things seldom are equal, and in that case, Sympathy, Knowledge, and the Truth outweigh all that the mixed school can offer.[24]

Many of the Southern schools where black teachers taught were dilapidated; supplies were limited, and books discarded from white schools were sent to black schoolchildren. Bernadine Morris describes one such school in Hampton, Virginia: "In one of the all-black schools where I taught whenever the temperature dropped down below thirty degrees or thirty-two degrees, we were cold. There were times when the principal had to move us from one side of the building and double up classes because it was so cold. How can you teach in a doubled-up situation?"

Etta Joan Marks, a soft-spoken teacher from Lindale, Texas, frowns as she recalls the abysmal conditions she endured in segregated schools: "In 1961 or 1962, when our school burned down, we didn't have textbooks of any kind. We held classes in the church. The white schools sent us their used textbooks just before they were ready to put them in the trash. Pages were torn out; they were old, worn, and so marked up that there wasn't any space to write our names."

Everett Dawson Jr. echoes these sentiments. "When people talk about separate but equal, I know what they were talking about. I know why they said the schools were inherently

---

[24] W. E. B. Du Bois, "Does the Negro Need Separate Schools?" *Journal of Negro Education* 4 (July 1935), pp. 328–35.

unequal, because I experienced it as a student and a teacher. In the black schools we only got the books that white kids had already used. They did not get books that we had used. In other words, we got the hand-me-downs. To this day it bothers me that those conditions existed anywhere in this country."

Black communities have a long tradition of having organized private schools for the benefit of their children. By teaching in private schools and establishing their own schools, black teachers have played a critical role in the creation of this educational infrastructure. Black teachers founded Sunday schools in the North in the late eighteenth century and native schools in the South prior to the end of the Civil War. They established several private schools in the South during the late nineteenth and early twentieth centuries. And they taught in schools established by black churches and organizations. Ruby Middleton Forsythe taught at Holy Cross Faith Memorial School, an Episcopal school, from 1938 until she retired in 1991. The school was founded in 1903 for the benefit of black children who lived on the rice plantations on Pawley's Island. "At the time there wasn't a public school for black children, not until later on. Once the public schools opened, they weren't fulltime. They only went for six months, but this school went for nine." When the Episcopal Diocese terminated the funding, the parents elected to keep the school open. Miss Ruby believes she knows the reason: "Regardless of what white people think about this school, the community thinks the school serves a good purpose. The parents don't want me to close the school. That's the reason we get the support that we do."

What was the price of desegregation? One price was paid by black children themselves. Anna Julia Cooper, a famous black educator of the late nineteenth and twentieth centuries, said she was opposed to desegregation because she feared that black children would no longer be taught racial pride as they had been in segregated schools.[25]

---

[25] Darlene Clark Hine, Elsa Barkley Brown, and Rosalyn Terborg-Penn, eds., *Black Women in America: An Historical Encyclopedia* (Bloomington: University of Indiana Press, 1993), p. 27.

Echoing these sentiments, Ruby Forsythe, an eighty-year-old teacher, discusses how integration has affected black pupils: "When the children were integrated into white schools, they lost something. Integration has helped in some ways, but it has hurt our black children in some ways. Now, instead of seeing black children winning prizes for their achievements, you see them all in special education classes. This has caused them to lose their pride, their self-esteem. They have been pushed back, as far as leadership is concerned. Instead of being taught to lead, they are being taught to follow."

Bernadine Morris agrees: "I think when they integrated the schools, instead of the black kids seeing themselves as people who could go in there and make progress, they got linked and then linked themselves to all the bad things that the kids were doing. I can only relate to when I was in a segregated school. You'd go to high school commencement and I could see these kids walking up there with these four-year scholarships to places like Fisk and Howard or A&T or wherever. Now when I go to a high school graduation, the only kids I see getting the scholarships are white kids."

Etta Joan Marks describes what happened to black pupils when they entered the desegregated schools in Lindale, Texas: "The teachers made it clear that blacks were not welcome. In the classroom, the white teachers would put the black kids on one side of the room and the white kids on the other side. This is so that they wouldn't touch or mingle."

Everett Dawson, who transferred to the desegregated school (after having taught in the segregated school) in the same community, was upset by the treatment of black kids: "I also saw a lot of young black brothers get into the classes of white instructors who went into the class saying — not saying very loudly but very clearly — 'These black kids can't make it.' And this really bothered me."

Bernadine B. Morris, one of the first black teachers to integrate the schools in Hampton, describes the way some white teachers treated black children: "Several times I had students who were acting up in the cafeteria, doing childlike things. These teachers wanted to make a federal case of it. They would say something like, 'He's still talking when I told him not to talk.' Well, this is what children do. I would always intervene and tell the teachers that I would take care of the problem. I had to do this, otherwise the teachers would make a big case out of nothing and then the children would get into trouble, be suspended or expelled. We had several white teachers in that school who retired rather than work with black children, which was fine. I felt like if they didn't want to teach black kids then they ought to leave."

How did desegregation affect black teachers? Predicting what might happen to black teachers, one black pundit declared that integration would jeopardize black teachers' security and undermine their morale. Not only would their livelihood be threatened, but their intellectual competence would also be called into question. Part of the problem lay in the *Brown* decision, which rested on the assumption that a school with an all-black faculty did not provide an education equal to that provided by an all-white faculty even if the buildings and equipment were superior. Some black teachers were underprepared and unable to compete. But many black teachers, especially those in large cities, had more academic training and longer years of service in the public schools than white teachers, who generally had more employment opportunities.[26]

Other voices from the black community tried to assure black teachers that they would not be adversely affected. Two editorials in the *Journal of Negro Education*, one written in the spring of 1951 and the other in the spring of 1953, grappled with how black teachers would be affected by desegregation. The 1951 editorial argued that there were not enough white teachers to replace black teachers in desegregated schools. But the editor concluded that even if school desegregation resulted in the loss of all of the 75,000 black teachers it would be offset by the elimination

---

[26] Nick Aaron Ford, "Consider the Negro Teacher," *From the Korean War to the Emergence of Martin Luther King, Jr.*, vol. 6 of *A Documentary History of the Negro People in the United States*, ed. Herbert Aptheker (1951; reprint, New York: Carol Publishing Group, 1990), pp. 387–91; "A Teacher Looks at Integration," in Aptheker, pp. 218–24.

of segregated schools. A 1953 editorial noting that desegregation had been accomplished in southern Illinois, Indiana, Arizona, New Mexico, and New Jersey without dire results for black teachers concluded:

> From an analysis of all available data, it seems unquestionable that the future status of the Negro public school teacher, under desegregated public schools, should not cause concern. Tenure laws in the District of Columbia and *seven* of the states involved are such that some two-fifths of the Negro teachers will be protected in their present position. And the teacher supply and demand situation means that even without tenure laws, as far as the elementary school is concerned it will be practically impossible to replace Negro teachers with white. While the situation as to high school teachers is not so overwhelmingly convincing as in the case of elementary school teachers, even here, tenure laws, the supply and demand picture and expanding enrollments make it highly questionable as to whether more than a few, if any Negro high school teachers could be replaced by white, even if there was an inclination do to so.[27]

Popular magazines such as *Ebony* also tried to reassure the black community that black teachers would not unfairly bear the brunt of desegregation. The November 1955 issue of *Ebony* acknowledged that 125 black Oklahoma teachers had lost their positions because of desegregation and that Oklahoma black leaders were predicting the loss of another 300 in the state. On a more hopeful note, *Ebony* listed several reasons why the South could not afford to relinquish its black teachers.[28] In other issues *Ebony* carried articles featuring black teachers in Phoenix who were teaching in white classes after the city integrated its schools.[29] Despite these reassurances, it became apparent in the

[27] Charles H. Thompson's editorial comment in *The Journal of Negro Education* 22, no. 2 (Spring, 1953).
[28] "Is There Hope for Negro Teachers? South Must Face Fact That to Scuttle Negro Educators Is to Wreck Its Schools," *Ebony* (November 1955), pp. 35–39.
[29] "Phoenix Keeps Its Negro Teachers: Colored Educators Teach White Classes in a City That Voluntarily Integrated Its Schools," *Ebony* (November 1956), pp. 97–100.

school districts that immediately desegregated that black teachers would pay some of the costs of the *Brown* decision.

As the school year opened in 1956, black leaders in Oklahoma, a state that desegregated almost immediately, were contemplating the dismissal of eighty-six black teachers the previous July and considering whether federal lawsuits were warranted. Both the NAACP and the Oklahoma Association of Negro Teachers believed that some of the dismissals were the result of racial discrimination. Nonetheless, the NAACP decided against filing suit until more evidence could be gathered to substantiate claims of discrimination.[30] Similar dismissals were reported in other border states (West Virginia, Kentucky, Texas, and Missouri).[31]

Not all black teachers lost their positions. Some were transferred to newly desegregated schools, not always with favorable outcomes. The case of Leslie R. Austin, a black teacher assigned to a desegregated high school in Lincoln County, Oklahoma, is one example. When the Wellston (Oklahoma) schools became one of the first districts to desegregate in 1955, it closed the all-black Dunbar School and transferred its ninety students to an all-white school. Four of the five black teachers were dismissed; only Austin, who had served as principal, was hired to teach in the desegregated school. Though he was considered "an excellent teacher," he was dismissed after three years. (When white parents objected to his disciplining their children, the discipline of his classes was assigned to white teachers, and Austin was subsequently dismissed for failing to maintain a disciplined classroom environment.) Although the Wellston public schools claimed that his dismissal was not the result of discrimination, the town's segregationists had vowed to "'get rid' of the Negro teacher" during the school board election, and many of the community's black residents believed Austin's firing was racially motivated.[32]

---

[30] "Negro Teachers Losing Position" *Pittsburgh Courier* (10 September 1956), p. 16.

[31] "462 Negro Teachers Out, Many Land in New Jobs," *Southern School News* 5 (May 1959), p. 10.

[32] "Faculty Integration Receives Setback with Disclosure of Teacher Firing," *Southern School News* 5 (May 1959), p. 10.

Some of the black teachers I interviewed described the harm done to black teachers as a result of desegregation. Etta Joan Marks describes what happened to the black teachers in Lindale, Texas: "There were only two black teachers in the school, my cousin and myself. Neither one of us had a class because the townspeople didn't want us teaching their lily-white kids. In spite of all the problems I encountered, I was more fortunate than many black teachers. Most of those that worked with me in the segregated school didn't have jobs. They lost their positions and had to look for new ones in other communities. Only four of the twelve black teachers were retained in the system. Besides my cousin and I, only two other teachers —the homemaking teacher and her husband, the principal— were reassigned."

Since many school districts employed various delaying tactics to avoid desegregating their schools for almost fourteen years, it took more than twenty years before a complete picture of the negative effects on black teachers could be ascertained. The first eleven years of desegregation were later found to have had devastating effects on the number of black teachers in the seventeen Southern and border states. In that period alone, more than 30,000 black teachers lost their jobs.[33] Attempting to explain the reasons for this wholesale dismissal of black teachers, a task force of the National Education Assocation reasoned:

> It is clear that in the past, Negro teachers were employed specifically and exclusively for the purpose of teaching Negro pupils in segregated schools. Segregated schools required segregated facilities. Since Negro teachers were employed to teach Negro pupils, there were relatively few positions for Negro teachers in a school system with few classes for Negroes. In a system with no classes for Negroes, there were simply no positions for Negro teachers. It has been, and still is, widely assumed by many school board members that Negroes, both students and teachers, are intellectually inferior. From this specious premise, it follows that "quality education" can be obtained only

---

[33] "Impact of the 1954 *Brown v. Topeka Board of Education* Decision on Black Educators," *The Negro Educational Review* 30, no. 4 (October 1979), pp. 217–32.

when schools, even after being integrated, remain in spirit and often in name "white schools." White schools are viewed as having no place for Negro teachers.[34]

Another hidden cost of desegregation was the loss of community. Bernadine B. Morris discusses one way this happened: "Busing at that time meant closing the schools in black neighborhoods and sending the black kids to the white areas. They closed all the black schools. Greenbriar School where I once worked is now a recreation center. Murrow Peak, a school that the black community fought to have built for twenty years, was closed even though it was fairly new. Then integration came. Now Murrow Peak is a police academy. These schools no longer exist because they were located in black neighborhoods. They built new schools in predominantly white neighborhoods rather than keep those in the black community. The idea was to get the schools out of black neighborhoods—and they did a good job of it."

Etta Joan Marks compares the treatment of black students in segregated and desegregated schools: "I've taught in a segregated school and a desegregated school in the same town. If I had to compare the experiences, I would say that in the black schools teachers had to do a lot more work, but our kids were appreciated more. In the white school we get more materials, we have more to work with, but we—blacks—aren't appreciated as much."

Everett Dawson sighed: "I got disillusioned with integration because I could not get to my people and tell them all the things that they needed to know."

A dispirited Bernadine B. Morris observes: "It saddens me that so many of our black kids today are doing so poorly, even after integration. It saddens me that integration didn't turn out to be everything we had hoped for."

As early as the middle of the nineteenth century, black teachers had organized for their own benefit. The Association of Colored Teachers was in operation in New York as early as 1841.

---

[34] National Education Association, "Task Force Survey of Displacement in Seventeen Southern States" (Washington, D.C., 1965).

This group had its own publications: the *New York Journal of Education* and the *Weekly Messenger*. The group held meetings devoted to their problems and the promotion of education for New York's black pupils.[35] Another organization was the American Teachers Association. Originally founded in 1904 as the National Association of Teachers in Colored Schools, the American Teachers Association with associated state chapters continued until 1965 when it was merged with the National Education Association. Bernadine Morris discusses some of their activities: "In both North Carolina and Virginia I also got involved in the Teachers Association. We had our own black teachers associations. Black and white teachers held separate yearly conventions on the same weekend, usually in the fall. In North Carolina, black teachers met in Raleigh. In Virginia, we met in Richmond. The white teachers met in a downtown hotel. But because we couldn't go into the hotels, we would gather at Virginia Union University. There were sessions and workshops on various topics: how to work with slow children or how to work with advanced students, all the newest trends. Professors, principals, and master teachers lectured, presented workshops, and conducted the sessions."

Unprotected by tenure, subject to dismissal by white-run school boards, and fearful for their physical safety, many black teachers, especially those in the South, refrained from political action. Yet other black teachers actively participated in black teachers' associations to secure equal pay. Long before the *Brown v. the Board of Education* case was filed, black teachers had begun challenging the dual pay scales in Southern states. Between 1900 and 1930 discrepancies between black and white teachers' salaries had gradually decreased in thirteen Southern states. In 1900, black teachers earned 45 percent of the salaries

---

[35] Their petition was signed by sixteen African-American teachers. "Call to Negro Teachers' Meeting, 1841," *From Colonial Times through the Civil War*, vol. 1 of *A Documentary History of the Negro People in the United States*, ed. Herbert Aptheker (1951; reprint, New York: Citadel Press, 1979), pp. 211–12.

of their white counterparts; by 1930, black teachers earned 69 percent of their white counterparts' salaries.[36]

When Thurgood Marshall set up his law practice in Baltimore in 1934, he set out to organize black teachers throughout the state of Maryland and attempted to secure plaintiffs to fight for salary equalization. In 1931–32, black teachers in Maryland were earning $1,211 per year while white teachers earned $1,589.[37] Even worse, black elementary school teachers were earning $339 less than white janitors. Because Maryland's black teachers were covered by tenure laws, they were less vulnerable to being fired than were teachers in other states. Even so, many of the black teachers in Maryland were fearful of losing their jobs, so Marshall raised money for a trust fund to aid teachers in case they were dismissed once the cases were filed. Three years later, Marshall expanded the salary equalization cases to North Carolina and Virginia. In 1939 Marshall won equal pay concessions from nine Maryland county school boards.

In Virginia, where black teachers were not protected by tenure laws, Marshall had more difficulty securing plaintiffs. He filed a case on behalf of Melvin O. Alston, a city high school teacher who was earning $921 per year, $279 less than white high school teachers in the same school district. When the Norfolk School Board refused to renew the plaintiff's contract, Marshall jointly filed the suit on behalf of the Norfolk Teachers Association and Alston to prevent the firing of other teachers. The plaintiffs lost the case, but the decision was overturned by the Fourth Circuit Court of Appeals in Richmond. When the Supreme Court refused to hear the case, under the law at least, black teachers were entitled to equal pay.

In spite of the Alston case, it was several years before many school districts in Virginia and other Southern states complied with the law. The South Carolina State Legislature refused to

---

[36] Leander L. Boykin, "The Status and Trend of Differentials Between White and Negro Teacher's Salaries in the Southern States, 1900–1946," *Journal of Negro Education* 18 (Winter 1949), pp. 40–47.

[37] Boykin, "Differentials Between Salaries," p. 42.

appropriate the funds necessary to equalize the salaries of black teachers, and black teachers had to bring suit. In the 1944–45 school year, black teachers in South Carolina earned only 57.8 percent as much as white teachers. In 1945 Judge Waring ordered the Columbia and Charleston (South Carolina) public schools to pay black teachers salaries equal to those of white teachers.[38] By 1947 most of the South Carolina city school districts were paying black and white teachers equal salaries, but in rural areas black teachers were still receiving unequal pay.[39] It wasn't until 1952, two years before the *Brown* decision, that the salaries of black and white teachers were equalized in Summerton County, South Carolina—the county of *Briggs v. Elliot*, one of the suits consolidated into the *Brown* case.

During the 1944–45, school year black teachers in Louisiana had earned approximately 50 percent of what white teachers earned.[40] It was not until 1948, after an eight-year struggle, that black teachers represented by Thurgood Marshall won a decision ordering the Louisiana State Board of Education to pay equal salaries to black and white teachers.[41] In the mid-forties, white teachers in Alabama earned 67.4 percent more than black teachers. Ruby Gainer, the president of the Jefferson County (Alabama) Teachers Association, filed a suit that initiated the struggle to equalize teachers' salaries in Alabama.[42]

It was ordinary black teachers like Alston and Gainer who, often in conjunction with their local teachers organizations, played critical roles in these struggles over salary equalization. In 1933, for instance, North Carolina black teachers received an announcement informing them of a mass meeting. One purpose

---

[38] Kluger, *Simple Justice*, pp. 185, 191, 197–99, 214–16, 297, 303, 532.

[39] Ibid., p. 16.

[40] Boykin, "Differentials Between Salaries," p. 46.

[41] "Louisiana Teachers Win Long Fight for Equal Pay," *Pittsburgh Courier* (7 August 1948), p. 4.

[42] Boykin, "Differentials Between Salaries," p. 47; "Noted Educator Ruby Gainer Resigns After Famed 49-Year Career," *Jet Magazine* (10 September 1984), p. 26.

of the meeting, to be held in Raleigh on October 29 in conjunction with a statewide meeting of the NAACP, was to protest unequal salaries.[43] The teachers were asked to attend the meeting and to encourage other teachers to attend. Although 2,005 blacks attended the Raleigh meeting, it is unclear how many of those in attendence were teachers.[44]

A retired North Carolina teacher recalls the importance of black teachers' organizations in equalizing salaries: "Through the leadership of the North Carolina Teachers' Association—that was the black teachers of North Carolina who had banded together in an association (now it's part of the North Carolina Association of Educators)—we organized and were able to bring enough pressure to get the salaries equalized. This happened around 1945 or 1946."

The writings of black teachers reveal that many teachers considered their pupils apt and intelligent learners, that they were committed and related well to students, and that they did not always try to imbue them with traits like tractability that so often characterized the teaching of white Northern schoolmistresses. This was often true despite class differences between the teachers and their students.[45]

In a letter printed in *The Liberator* in 1862, Charlotte Fortune, a black teacher, described her pupils in the Reconstruction era:

It is very pleasant to see how bright, how eager to learn many of the children are. Some of them make wonderful improvement in a short

---

[43] "Black Teachers in the South: Negro Teachers' Salary," in *From the New Deal to the End of World War II*, vol. 4 of *A Documentary History of the Negro People in the United States*, ed. Herbert Aptheker (1951; reprint, New York: Citadel Press, 1979), pp. 37–39.

[44] George W. Streator, "The Colored South Speaks for Itself," in *From Colonial Times through the Civil War*, vol. 1 of *A Documentary History of the Negro People in the United States*, ed. Herbert Aptheker (1951; reprint, New York: Citadel Press, 1979), pp. 40–45.

[45] Jacqueline Jones, *Soldiers of Light and Love: Black Women, Work, and the Family from Slavery to the Present* (NY: Basic Books, 1985) , p. 138; see also chapter 5, pp. 109–139.

time. It is a great happiness, a great privilege to be allowed to teach them. Every day I enjoy it more and more.... They are certainly not the stupid degrading people that many in the North believe them to be.[46]

Another black teacher, Lucy Laney Craft, in a speech given at the turn of the century, criticized teachers who were ineffective with black pupils and called on black teachers to undertake their education:

> There's plenty of work for all who have the proper conception of the teacher's office.... But the educated Negro woman must teach the "Black Babies." But alas! These dull teachers, like many modern pedagogues and school keepers, failed to know their pupils—to find out their real needs, and hence had no cause to study methods of better and best development of the boys and girls under their care.[47]

One of the most insightful accounts about black pupils was written by Sara Stanley, who described the visit a government official paid to her classroom. The official was trying to convince her black pupils that whites were superior to them because of their education, but he was startled when the pupils insisted that if whites were better than they were, it was only because whites were richer and had stolen their money from black people:

> "Now, children," said he, "you don't think white people are any better than you because they have straight hair and white faces?"
>
> "No, sir," cried the children with intuitive comprehension of the great words uttered by Paul on Mars's hill.
>
> "No, they are not better, but they are different; they possess great power; they formed this great government; they control this vast country; they invent telegraphs and steamboats; they construct railroads and war steamers. Now, what makes them different from you?"
>
> The answer, "Education," seemed inevitable; but, instead a chorus of little voices instantly responded, "MONEY."
>
> "Yes," said the speaker, "but what enabled them to obtain it? *How* did they get that money?"
>
> A simultaneous shout burst forth, "Got it off us; stole it off we all."

---

[46] In Bert James Lowenberg & Ruth Bogin, eds., *Black Women in Nineteenth Century America: Their Words, Their Thoughts, Their Feelings* (University Park: Pennsylvania State University Press, 1976), pp. 294–95.
[47] Ibid., p. 297.

This teacher, admiring her pupils for their childlike honesty and sagacious insight, concluded the article by writing, "A different answer might have been returned, but hardly a truer one as applied to the people of the South."[48]

The teachers interviewed for this book echo the views of turn-of-the-century schoolmistresses. Mabel Bettie Moss, a teacher in Philadelphia, complains: "Most teachers don't appreciate black children and their strengths. Black kids are creative, inquisitive, and bright. That's the best word to describe them. . . . in so many instances school is just so boring and unrelated to their everyday lives. Occasionally when I have gone into other teachers' rooms, and seen what is going on, I have realized how awful it would be to have to be a student in that classroom. Too many teachers make learning so boring."

A novice male elementary teacher, Leonard Collins, agrees on the importance of making school relevant to his pupils' lives: "I put Africans within the context of everything that I teach. I do this with other cultures as well. For example, when I taught about the transcontinental railroad, I showed my class how Asians were exploited, how they were denigrated during this whole process. I try to show what role each group has played throughout history. I do this in anything that I teach but especially in social studies. By simply presenting the perspectives of people of color, I believe I am making a contribution. The only thing I can do is teach my kids to question authority, question what the teacher says, not to be submissive."

In segregated schools where black and white teachers made up the faculties, some black teachers complained of low expectations for and prejudice against black students. A history of Chicago public schools noted that too often white teachers made few academic demands of black students. One black teacher commented that the black students who came to her class were often lacking in grade-level skill: "The worst cases

---

[48] Ellen Nickenzie Lawsen with Marlene D. Merrill, *The Three Sarahs: Documents of Antebellum College Women* (New York: Edwin Mellen Press, 1984), p. 61.

I had came from children who had been pampered by white teachers interviewed in this book."[49]

A retired Chicago high school teacher, Leroy Lovelace, reports: "Teachers have to realize that black students—or all students, but I'm talking about black students now—are very clever, especially with white teachers. Too many black students have learned to play the game, to play on a teacher's sympathy in order to get away with doing nothing. Teachers have to demand from black urban students the same as they wouldwelcome datacomp demand from privileged white students, and they have to be consistent. Urban black students can do the work, and in the hands of skilled teachers they will do it. They may have to work harder to achieve success. All students can con teachers if the teachers let themselves be conned. But it's often easier for black students to con white teachers because the students know that the teachers will pity them, feel sorry for them, and make excuses that these students can't do this, can't do that or that there's a problem at home. It particularly disturbs me when I see black teachers letting black students get away with doing nothing. Black teachers who do this tell themselves they are doing this sympathetically, but I don't accept that. I believe that black teachers are doing it because we've become middle-class—and now I am speaking of black folks including black teachers. Once black folks were poorer than Job's turkey and now that we have joined the white folks talking about 'They can't do it.'—you'd be surprised how many black teachers do that."

Not all black teachers are sympathetic to their young scholars. Color distinctions between light-skinned black teachers and their dark-complexioned pupils were sometimes enacted in the classroom with teachers favoring lighter pupils over darker ones. *The Chicago Defender* editor, Robert Abbott, himself a dark-complexioned man, complained,

> The pure-blooded, black children are seldom if ever the recipients of kindly counsel or special favors or justifiable considerations. We can neither, nor appreciate Race teachers who manifest no interest in, no

---

[49] Homel, *Down from Equality*, p. 110.

sympathy and no consideration for those children of ours who show no sign of racial admixture. We resent it and decry it the more when Race teachers, who should be the last ones to exhibit aversion to their kind, practice the most objectionable form of partiality on the basis of color.

One black parent whose child was failing in school denounced her black teachers, "You colored teachers just don't like Mattie Lou cause she's black and ain't got good hair."[50]

Millicent Byard Gray is familiar with the attitudes about color that often permeate the black community: "The teachers at Lincoln High School were black but for the most part they were light-skinned. There was a lot of color consciousness in my community and in my school. I'm the brown-skinned child, one of the darkest children in my family. Even as child, I was serious. The neighbors used to comment, 'That little dark one — she's too serious; we need to watch her — she doesn't laugh when the rest of them laugh.' In those days people equated being dark skinned with being evil. I always resented that."

These teachers agonize over the disintegration of urban and rural black communities, the rampant materialism of the society, and the devastating effect these conditions have had on the pupils they teach. Joelle Vanderall describes her school community: "Many of my students come from neighborhoods that are devastated, communities in which drugs are rampant, where people haven't got the money they need to survive and they see no way out. Before, black people had more stability, jobs, and some hope. But now welfare has created a permanent class of expendable people without hope who can always be used as scapegoats by the politicians and the larger society."

A Philadelphia teacher, Mabel Bettier Moss, discusses the changes she has witnessed in the community surrounding her school: "I have been teaching in this community—in the same school—since 1961, and I can really see the negative effect that drugs have had on the community. The way things are going, it's only going to get worse. In the late eighties, we had a drug house right across from our school. With the grip that crack cocaine has

---

[50] Ibid., p. 111.

on our community, a lot of the mothers are simply unable to cope. Crack cocaine is so cheap, and it grabs them so fast. In this community, more and more grandmothers are raising their grandchildren, and although many of them do a fantastic job, others are simply too worn out to raise another generation. One little girl in my class last year is being raised by her grandmother, a sickly woman, who has six children under twelve in her home, from three different daughters, all victims of crack cocaine."

A Southern teacher, Bernadine Morris, who earlier in her career taught in rural communities and once lived in a "teacher-age" (a boarding house for teachers), remembers how living and participating in the daily life of the community cemented relationships between parents and teachers: "In Warrenton, teachers were respected by children and their families. I remember several Christmases, when even though the families didn't have money to go out and buy the teacher a gift, the children would come to school with gifts, something that their families had raised. If you'd go to the home, the parents would often invite you back to dinner. They would notify you if their children were involved in various church activities and invite you to come and see. The supportive relationships between black teachers and parents aren't like they used to be. And as a result children, black children, are suffering."

A Washington, D.C., high school teacher, Lerone Swift, places some of the blame for the disintegration of the community at the feet of the black middle class. He blames them for turning their backs on poor blacks: "middle-class parents have abandoned the school system that benefited them, that provided them with the opportunity to advance and become successful in society."

Whereas in 1974, historically black colleges, which had prepared the majority of black teachers, graduated approximately nine thousand teachers, ten years later they were graduating only half as many. By the end of the 1980s, a number of policy analysts were examining the reasons for the shortage and projected shortages of black teachers, whose numbers were in sharp decline. Black college students were no longer choosing teaching as a career. Some of the other reasons for this decline include the increased reliance on standardized tests for acceptance into and graduation from teacher training programs; the lower number of black students enrolling in and completing four-year colleges; and the expanded occupational choices available to black college graduates.[51] Because the number of black teachers had become so small and was projected to remain insignificant, some referred to them as an "endangered species." According to the 1990 census black teachers represented only 8 percent of all teachers.[52] Their numbers were declining at exactly the same time that black students comprised the majority in many urban school districts. To offset this imbalance, numerous programs were being developed and launched to recruit more black teachers into the profession. But the predictions for increasing the number of black teachers were bleak.

Although the older teachers interviewed for this book have spent their entire professional lives as teachers, the younger teachers were not likely to do the same. The day after I interviewed Leonard Collins in California, he was flying to the East Coast to visit a graduate program in African-American studies that he hoped to enter in the fall of 1997. Another young teacher, Ashallah Williams, says: "For me teaching is one of the first of many careers."

Black teachers' unique historical experiences are either completely overlooked or amalgamated with those of white teachers. In those few instances where black teachers are visible, their cultural representations are biased by society's overarching racism. For the most part, these cultural representations continue to render black teachers invisible as teachers of students of their own or of other ethnic backgrounds, while casting white female teachers as heroic figures. It is perhaps emblematic of this phenomenon that two of the most recent books about effective teachers of

---

[51] Michele Foster, "African-American Teachers and Culturally Relevant Pedagogy," in *Handbook of Research on Multicultural Education*, ed. James Banks (New York: Macmillan Press, 1995), pp. 2132–82.

[52] Census of Population and Housing 1990: Equal Employment Opportunity (EEO) File on CD-Rom [Machine Readable Data Files]/Prepared by the Bureau of the Census: Washington, D.C.: The Bureau [Publisher and Distributor], 1992.

black and Latino students in New York and in California are *Small Victories* and *My Posse Don't Do Homework*,[53] the latter currently appearing as a movie entitled *Dangerous Minds*. Both books depict white, not black, female teachers negotiating the difficult terrain of urban classrooms.

The public rarely reads about black teachers like Mamie Williams, an exemplary teacher who taught in the segregated schools of Topeka, Kansas:

> Mamie Williams became a master teacher. A forceful taskmaster and disciplinarian, she was no ogre. Her classroom was never a place for rote learning, and she readily acknowledged that "children with their sincerity and candor can teach adults something new every day." She was a great one for mottos. One of her favorites was: "Life is infinitely rich in fine and adequate compensations. Never a door is shut but several windows are opened." Mamie Williams was a window-opener. She designed several projects of the kind she had heard about at Columbia. One of the most popular was a communal lesson in self-government: the whole school was organized like a state, with a constitution, by-laws, officers, and a legislative council. There were campaign speeches and elections, rousing inauguration ceremonies, and regular legislative reports to be filed and posted on the bulletin board in every classroom. She organized a "Little Theater," a project for which her pupils dramatized stories they had read together in class. One time, she turned her classroom into an art gallery; those who liked to draw contributed their work, the others brought in what they liked from magazines and other sources, and every one was excited and stimulated and learned how widely human notions of beauty can vary.[54]

The shrinking numbers of black teachers have compelled me to publish these contemporary accounts by black teachers. In the pages that follow, teachers talk about the racism in segregated and desegregated schools, the repeated cycles of attempted and aborted reform efforts, and the different perceptions of black and white teachers about the ability and needs of black students, parents, and communities. Much of what these

---

[53] Samuel G. Freedman, *Small Victories: The Real World of a Teacher, Her Students and Their High School* (New York: Harper & Row, 1990); Louanne Johnson, *My Posse Don't Do Homework* (New York: St Martin's Press, 1995).

[54] Kluger, *Simple Justice*, p. 378.

teachers say is controversial. Nonetheless, it is my hope that these accounts will provide a voice for an historically marginalized group, that in the process they will enhance our capacity to understand the experiences of black teachers, and that they will assist contemporary and future African-Americanists, historians, and sociologists in reaching a more complete understanding of education, schooling, teaching, and learning in the United States.

Part I

THE ELDERS

EVERETT DAWSON

He is serene, philosophical, and soft-spoken. His melodious Southern accent is so muted, it is often difficult to understand. Nonetheless, his sense of humor is evident. Everett Dawson was born and raised in Pittsboro, a rural North Carolina community. An able student, he received a double promotion, completing seventh and eighth grades in one year. After graduating from North Carolina A&T in 1943, he returned home to teach. Now retired from the school system, he continues to work with students in the University of North Carolina Upward Bound Program in Chapel Hill. A deeply religious man, he is a lifelong member of the AME Church.

I taught forty-one years in the same school system. After integration took place I was still in the same system but not the same school. I taught at the all-black school, Horton, for twenty-seven years; from 1943 to 1970 I was in the same school, half that time in the same room. In 1970 the schools in Pittsboro, North Carolina, were integrated. When the schools were integrated, nine or ten of us went to Northwoods, the high school. I taught there for fourteen years.

Horton contained all grades, one through twelve. I was a student at Horton, and after graduation, I returned there to teach. Quite a few of the teachers who were there when I was in high school were still there when I returned. The man who was principal when I graduated was still there. The teacher who suggested that I be moved from seventh to eighth grade was still there. The teacher who coached students—boys and girls—in basketball was still there. A lot of people say that women shouldn't be coaching. But she coached, and had some good boys' teams.

I didn't really have any problems working with my former teachers. We got along very well as teachers. We didn't have any real problems. None of them ever said, "Well, I taught you, so therefore you must listen to me." That attitude did not exist. They helped me and hopefully I helped them. But I don't know what they said when they got behind closed doors.

Today I look back and see the inequity in equipment, books, and materials in the black schools. When people talk about separate but equal, I know what they were talking about. I know why they said the schools were inherently unequal, because I experienced it as a student and a teacher. In the black schools we only got the books that white kids had already used. They did not get books that we had used. In other words, we got the hand-me-downs. To this day it bothers me that those conditions existed anywhere in this country.

Another condition that existed in black schools is that the teachers had to be able to pitch in and teach whatever needed to be taught. When I came back from college to teach at Horton in 1943, I had to teach everything. People sometimes ask me what I taught at Horton. And I have to tell them I taught—or I tried to teach—everything. I won't say I taught because sometimes I'm not sure whether I was teaching or just experimenting. But while I was at Horton, I taught history—actually, social studies—geography, sociology, economics, all of those subjects, at one time or another. Also I taught health and physical education as well as math and some science. In a small town, there wasn't much choice. There weren't enough teachers to cover all the subject matters.

When I look back to when I first started teaching, the one thing that has bothered me all these years is that black teachers were not paid the same rate as whites in North Carolina. So where black teachers were getting, like, $90 a month, white teachers were getting about $120 a month. This is a guess because I never did know the exact salary scale. At this time

teachers didn't make very much money. Through the leadership
of the North Carolina Teachers Association—that was the black
teachers of North Carolina who had banded together in an association (now it's part of the North Carolina Association of Educators)—we organized and were able to bring enough pressure to
get the salaries equalized. This happened around 1945 or 1946.
The salaries weren't very high, but at least they were equal. All of
the teachers, black and white, were making the same salary with
the same certification. They didn't give us any back pay. I feel
that somewhere down the line somebody owes me some money.

Even so when I was a student the teachers at my high school
did a remarkable job with what they had. First of all, they had a
bunch of children who, in general, did not have access to public
libraries, who did not take newspapers, who did not have magazines coming into their homes. There were a few exceptions, but
basically most of the students didn't come from such homes. With
what they had in the way of supplies and materials and the preparation of the students, they did a remarkable job. As I look back
and see where we came from, I am amazed at what the teachers
who taught me were able to do with their students. This is not
only on the high school level but even at the college level.

A lot of people say that the teaching in all-black schools wasn't
up to par, but I disagree with that because I saw and experienced
the good work we were able to do with black students. I often
wonder if white folks really want black kids to be successful. I
started the first advanced math class in Chatham County; this was
at Horton, the all-black, segregated school. The advanced math
class was a course where they got beyond geometry and algebra
two. But when the county school officials found out what we were
doing, they blocked the course. They cut it out until the white
school could establish the course and catch up with us. That's how
determined the white folks were to be better than we were.

Before I went to college, I considered agriculture. But having
grown up on a farm and plowed and picked cotton, I decided I
had seen enough of mules. By the time I went to North Carolina
A&T, I had become interested in medicine, my first love. I wanted
to be a doctor because I remember when my biological mother

died at twenty-three it affected me so much that I decided to become a doctor in order to cure disease so that nobody would have to die like my mother did. But I have always had a palsy-like condition; my hands shake a lot. I figured that my physical condition would not allow me to be a doctor; I couldn't handle the needles and measuring medicines so I ruled that out on my own.

Since math was my next love, I decided to major in math. After I got into mathematics, my foster mother insisted that I become a teacher. After graduation, I was called into the military service. Although I failed the physical, I got this letter from the War Department asking me to come to Washington to work with computers. But I couldn't do that because I promised my mother I was going to teach, that I would try to get a teaching job. When I was offered the teaching job, I jumped on it. If I hadn't gotten a job, I would have probably wound up in computers working for the government. I have no regrets, except that had I gone to Washington I would have been more rewarded financially and might have avoided all these years wrestling with these hardheaded kids. That's how I wound up being a teacher. It was not because I loved teaching that much. In fact, I didn't start loving teaching until I'd been in it, maybe, about ten years, once I started seeing where I was making a difference.

I think I made a difference in the lives of black children. It wasn't until after I began working at Northwoods that I became disillusioned with what I saw in desegregated schools. The biggest difference is that we were able to do more with the black students in all-black schools. In other words, if I wanted to I could come in this morning and have my children put their books under the desk or on top of the desk while I sit on top of my desk and ask: "Why are you here? Are you here just to make out another day? Are you here because the law says you must go to school? Are you here to try to better yourself? Do you know where your competition is? Your competition is not your little cousin sitting over there. Your competition is that little white kid sitting over in the other school. He's the one you have got to compete with for a job. And the only way that you're going to get that job is that you are going to have to be better than he is."

I could talk to them about this kind of thing. I could drill this into their heads.

Once you integrated, and had mixed groups, I didn't feel comfortable getting into the things the whites did to us as black people because I know how I felt when they talked about me. I got disillusioned with integration because I could not get to my people and tell them all the things that they needed to know. I couldn't beat into their minds that to compete with a white kid on an equal basis was not enough. I also saw a lot of young black brothers get into the classes of white instructors who went into the class saying—not saying very loudly but very clearly — "These black kids can't make it." And this really bothered me.

Looking back at the way desegregation was handled, I should have known there were going to be problems for black students. In 1970 they paid all of us teachers—black and white—to attend a three-day workshop because we were preparing to integrate the school. The first day of the workshop we had these so-called experts who were supposed to know everything. Essentially, they told the white teachers what they could expect from the black students. They told them not to expect black students to come to class and say, "Yes ma'am," and "No, ma'am." These experts told the white teachers that even though they were used to being addressed politely by their students, the black students weren't going to be polite. They told the white teachers that black students were not going to bring in all their homework every day. They went on and on about what black students weren't going to do, and what the white teachers were going to have to accept from the black students once the schools were integrated. We spent the entire first day—six hours—listening to these experts tell white teachers how to get along with the black child.

The second day we spent the entire six hours listening to the experts tell the white teachers how to get along with the black kids. On the third day, we were still listening to the experts telling these white teachers how to get along with black kids.

After we came back from lunch break on the third day, they started in saying the same things. I was angry, so I stood up and said, "We have spent two and a half days here and all you have done is tell these white teachers how to get along with these black kids. You have not told me how to get along with white kids. You got some of them out there just as difficult as any black child. These white children are not going to come into the classroom and be little angels. They are children, just like the black children. But you have not said anything to me about how I am supposed to deal with the white child. Why was the white teacher told how to deal with the problems he was going to have with the black kids? When I was a youngster, fortunately or unfortunately, my parents drilled into me "When you go to Miss Ann's house, you go to the back door and knock." Now I've got this little white kid in my class who is going to try and run me out and I am not going anywhere. Now I have to go visit that parent. You haven't told me whether I should I go to the back door, the front door, or the side door."

What they were saying, as far as I was concerned, is that as a white person you are going to have trouble with black kids. That white kid is going to give teachers problems too. Now, I had taught black kids and I knew that some of them could be problems because I had my share of problems with some of them, and I am black. But don't tell me that because he's black that he's automatically going to be a problem. And that the white child, because he's white, is not going to be a problem. You are going to have some problems with white kids.

When we really got into integration, I found out that most of the drugs, 90 percent, that came onto the campus at Northwoods came from white kids. Every once in a while a little black kid would get his hands on a few ounces of this or that, that he might distribute. But the basic problem did not come from us; it came from someone else. And that's one of the things that we as black people allowed to happen. We didn't challenge their views about our black children.

Working in an integrated high school gave me a chance to see how desegregation discriminated against and pigeonholed black teachers and students. When we were integrated, I went in not only as a teacher but as a coach. Never mind that I was never involved in any athletics in college, I wound up coaching football, basketball, and baseball. The assistant coach was also black. I guess they thought that black men should be coaches. Even though I had never played any sports, I did do a good job, even if I do say so myself. Of course, I had to read a lot of books, watch a lot of films, and attend a lot of games in order to be able to do the job.

I remember being assigned to teach a course for students who were difficult: black students who weren't supposed to be good at academics. I developed a course I called applied mathematics. What I did was make everything in the course apply to the real world. I asked how many of the students were interested in brick masonry and there were about six. All the work they were assigned in this class was based on brick masonry: how to calculate money, how to calculate the cost of material, even how to figure out your income tax. For those who were interested in carpentry, everything in the course was connected with carpentry in some way. They learned how to measure off a room, how to read a blueprint, and other practical things. There were four categories, some in auto mechanics and the rest in computers. The course was algebra, but all the algebra was linked to students' interests. The students in that class didn't cause any trouble. On any given day someone could walk by that room and almost hear a pin drop, because all the students were interested in what they were doing. But the very next year the administration cut the class out because those kids were doing too well. They weren't causing any trouble and they were interested in school.

Again, what black kids miss as a result of desegregation is the serious kind of conversations that we were able to have in all-black schools. Black kids are not hungry now. There are some few that want to be on top, but they are not really hungry. If they want to be on top, they want to be there because they heard someone say that it is nice. But they do not hunger and thirst after righteousness, if I can use that expression from the Bible. They don't hunger and thirst for education. And the reason they don't hunger is because nobody tells them that they need to hunger and thirst for education. Once they went into the integrated situation there was no one pushing them. They looked at Martin

Luther King who said, "I have seen the Promised Land." Now that black children are in integrated schools, they say, "I have reached the Promised Land. Now that I am here I don't have to be concerned."

Black adults are partly to blame for the plight of the black child. The adults in the black community did not like what was going on in the society. Because we didn't like what was going on, we decided to do whatever it took to knock down the walls of segregation. So we got our hammers and knocked on the wall until it fell. But then once we got the wall down we said, "Children, walk over into the Promised Land. Now you go on in the Promised Land, and we are going to stay right here." Our children got to the Promised Land and we stayed on our side of the wall. We never went there and told them how we could help. We simply got them into the situation, but we didn't help them learn how to live in that situation. As adults who didn't come up in that environment, I don't think we realize what we have done to black children. It's like taking a baby and standing him out there on Franklin Street and leaving him there: "Well, now that you're on Franklin Street, you have to make it." We just let them walk into the lion's jaw without supporting them. One of the things that the black community needs to do now is to turn inward to give our children more help. Once we were able to get into the University of North Carolina and other integrated settings, we stopped. We need to use our churches to provide support for our children— buy some computers, put them in the basement, teach our children history, mathematics, computers, science. We can't tell our children, "I've got mine, now all you have to do is go get it." It's just not that easy.

My greatest strength as a teacher is that I am able to communicate with students. The ultimate end in teaching is being able to communicate and get your point across to those individuals you teach. My philosophy of education has been never to give up on a child, because I figured that if you work with him long enough and hard enough that eventually he will come around. A lot of people have told me that that is a bad philosophy. I am beginning to reassess my philosophy because I have learned that it doesn't necessarily follow that if you work with some kids for ten years that they are going to turn around. But I have had more successes than failures. So, although I've modified my philosophy somewhat, I have confidence in the abilities of black youngsters. I enjoy working with Upward Bound because once again, in addition to teaching mathematics, I have the opportunity to get to my people to talk to them and tell them all the important things that I used to preach to black children when I taught in segregated schools. It's as if I have come back home.

ORA BENSON

The child of immigrant parents from Jamaica, West Indies,
Ora Benson was born in New York City in 1911. As the child
of immigrants, she lived in a close-knit West Indian commu-
nity, but at the same time she encountered the multicultural-
ism that characterized New York City between the 1880s and
the 1920s. When I first contacted her for an interview she
graciously refused because she was recovering from an ill-
ness. When I contacted her a few years later, she agreed. The
two interviews from which this narrative is taken were con-
ducted in her home in Point Richmond, California, which
overlooks San Francisco Bay.

Most people are shocked when they learn that I was a Latin teacher,
perhaps because they don't expect a black woman to be a Latin
teacher. I always wanted to teach Latin, but when I graduated in
1933 the City of New York had other thoughts. Even though I had
prepared myself to teach Latin, it wasn't until thirty-two years later,
in 1965 when my husband took a job in Richmond, California, that I
finally got to teach it and then I was mostly teaching white students.
On the long journey to teaching Latin, I had lots of experiences
which I now value, because they taught me something about
myself, forced me to re-examine some of the values I learned in my
family, and cemented my relationship to the black community.

When I finished Hunter College in 1933 with my major in
Latin, there was nothing to teach. The City of New York fooled

me, and everybody else, because they eliminated Latin from the course of study in the public schools when we were juniors in college. In fact, we didn't get a chance to present ourselves with any credentials because they had stopped giving exams during the Depression years. We had to pass an examination to get a license, but instead of receiving a permanent license we were issued substitute licenses. With a substitute's license, you could get day-to-day work. That's what we did. There were no permanent teachers assigned during the Depression. I was fortunate enough to be qualified to get both a high school and elementary school license. I knew I wasn't going to be able to teach Latin; I would have to teach elementary school, and I felt fortunate to be able to teach elementary school when I could, which I did as a day-to-day substitute.

Not too much later the city became concerned about the problem of reading. Since I had taken courses in reading at Hunter, when the city established the program to improve the reading skills of elementary school students, I applied for that and was able to get a job teaching in the remedial reading program. The program was funded by the WPA, the Works Progress Administration.[55] Our group was the first to start the program in the city. I learned a great deal. We would meet regularly—every other week or every week—with a woman who was in charge of the

---

[55] In New York City WPA assisted white-collar workers as well as blue-collar workers. WPA in New York City was organized into four divisions. One of these divisions responsible for white-collar and service activities was the Women's and Professional Projects, which encompassed six departments: Education, Research and Statistical Records, Clerical, Hospital and Health, Recreation and Production and Service. Education projects were sponsored by the New York Board of Education. Although most of the education activities were directed at adults, other education activities included remedial reading in elementary and secondary schools, assistance in handling truancy, extracurricular activities or field trips to museums, instruction for homebound children and vocational guidance for junior and senior high school students. According to a report issued in May 1937, the number of workers employed in the Education Department was 8,681, the largest number after Production and Service. John David Millett, *The Works Progress Administration in New York City* (Chicago: Public Administration Service, 1938) pp. 68, 105-126.

program. We'd talk about the goals of the program, the materials that we were using. We'd discuss them, try them out, and report back to her on the efficacy of each item, each exercise.

The first school I was assigned to was overcrowded, just like a lot of schools in the city then. It was at 127th Street and St. Nicholas Avenue, near the park. It was so crowded that I taught my first class in the basement of the school. But I didn't care. I was so happy to have a regular job. I got paid every week, just $28.76, or something like that, but I could look forward to a steady income. This was Harlem in the early thirties, during the Depression, and I was lucky to have a job in the teaching profession, because that is when a lot of people—professional black people—had to take menial jobs if they could find any job at all. So I worked on this job under the auspices of WPA for about three or four years. Then I got another job. WPA was beginning to fold up; it was the end of the thirties and things were beginning to get a little better.

At that time they were developing special schools in the city, and I became involved with the Children's Aid Society in New York, a very large social services organization. They had been given money to organize some special schools for youngsters who had problems at home and at school. The Children's Aid Society decided that if children could be helped as quickly as possible after a disastrous experience that might be the way to save some children. Through the Children's Aid Society I got the job of being the teacher at one of their centers. The center was outside of New York City in a place called Wallkill, about ninety miles from the city. The Children's Aid Society had a camp beside the Wallkill River, and the Catskills were way off in the distance. It was a lovely, lovely spot, and on their property they had an old farmhouse, which was several hundred years old. The house was so solidly built that with a little interior renovation it became a school and a home for girls.

The Children's Aid Society decided to start a pilot program in which they would work with not more than fifteen girls at a time. There was a staff—a housemother, a cook and her husband, who was also the chauffeur and handyman. Every week, if the weather wasn't bad, a Children's Aid social worker came to visit. I was assigned the job of being the teacher there. I taught the girls everything that they were weak in, although I emphasized reading.

I went up to this place with a great deal of anticipation and yet some trepidation, because I had not had too much experience with so-called "bad" girls. I was assured these weren't really bad girls. These girls had just gotten into difficulty. They had problems of one sort or another, and had gotten in trouble for the first time. They were all upper elementary school-age youngsters.[56] A few of them were bigger than I was. Many of them had lived difficult lives and they were all more experienced than I in living. As the child of immigrants, I had lived a sheltered life; I also had very fixed ideas about how people should behave. Although I wasn't always conscious of it, I am sure I was judgmental about how people ought to live, what they ought to think, and how they ought to behave. In the beginning I was determined to save these girls, to help make them into my own image of respectability. As I got to know them I tried to imagine myself at their ages, ten or twelve, having experienced what these children had been through. Eventually, I learned to see life from their perspective and I tried to help them see life from mine. We learned about each other and from each other.

The Wallkill years were the beginning of a self-examination into my own background and its effect on my own values. My parents were from Jamaica, the West Indies. They were immigrants who came to the United States in the early part of the century when many people were beginning to feel that they had to get out for better opportunities—seeking the "American Dream." Although they knew each other in Jamaica, they came separately, mother first. They got married in 1910, or 1909, and I was born in 1911. As I grew up, I heard stories about life in Jamaica. People who had just arrived from the West Indies frequently stayed at our house before they settled elsewhere. My brother and I

---

[56] See Carlton Mabee, *Black Education in New York State. From Colonial to Modern Times* (Syracuse: Syracuse University, 1979), p. 254, for a discussion of the schools and camps run by the New York Children's Aid Society.

looked forward to their visits because usually they'd bring something from Jamaica, a mango or a coconut.

We lived like the typical immigrant family. My parents associated only with other Jamaicans; they would tolerate Barbadians,
Trinidadians, and other West Indians. At the time, I don't even
remember realizing that I was black. We were Jamaicans, West
Indians; we were foreigners.

Harlem was the transition area for foreigners. At that time,
most blacks lived in the lower part of the city. Since we seldom
went to the lower part of the city and there were practically no
blacks in Harlem at that time, I had little contact with native-born
blacks. My parents' first apartment in Harlem was on 132nd
Street between Second and Lenox Avenue. In those days, my parents and the other adults I knew were rather arrogant; they
looked down on other black people. When I was a child it was
difficult for black men to get good jobs and throughout his life
my father had very low-level jobs; he struggled and took whatever he could get. But he still thought of himself and his family
as respectable.

Respectability meant a lot of things. It meant that my mother
was not allowed to work even though we desperately needed the
money. In my father's book, wives did not work if you were
respectable. Wives were supposed to stay home and take care of
the children, and that's what my mother did. He was an immigrant; he wanted to be seen as very respectable, so his wife did
not work. Respectability dictated how children were raised and
how they conducted themselves in public. He had lots of other
ideas about what it meant to be respectable, and since I was
immersed in that immigrant family and that immigrant community, a lot of those ideas about respectability rubbed off on me.

It wasn't until I went to Wardleigh High School for girls that I
met girls from American-born black families. We didn't do much
home visiting. We were mostly school friends because my home-
life was still closed. Every school year we'd renew our friendships
and walk home together. Two of the girls with whom I was quite
friendly were daughters of the man who was the head of the
NAACP at that time, and another was the daughter of a family con-

nected to the Urban League. So even my association with black Americans was limited to those from a certain class background.

Despite the snobbish attitudes I was learning from my family and community, my interest in Latin also was fostered by my experiences as the child of immigrants. Church was a very important aspect of our life. Most of the people who we met at church were from Barbados, St. Kitts, or someplace else in the West Indies; our church was a meeting place. It enabled them to feel at home, to find out about jobs, to discuss their mutual problems, and to learn how to deal with them. It was at church at St. Ambrose that I first became interested in Latin. Our prayer books had the first phrase of every psalm in Latin. I used to wonder what the words meant. When I asked my parents, they didn't know. They knew it was Latin but not what the words meant. When we asked the minister, he told us it was Latin, taught us how to pronounce the words, and what they meant in English. That's how I became familiar with Latin and became interested in studying it. When I went to junior high school and learned that one could take Latin I decided I was going to take it. My fascination with the language stayed with me and I took Latin in junior high school, in high school, and majored in it at Hunter College.

My desire to be a teacher came from several sources. In my father's family, there were many teachers. As a child I heard my father talk about his brothers who were teachers. My mother used to tell us these wonderful stories about her teachers in Jamaica—Teacher Brown and Teacher Wilson and so on; they called their teachers "Teacher." There was also a pretty large group of young women who attended my church who were in college studying to be teachers and others who inspired me to continue studying to become a teacher because they had become teachers in New York.

But the one person in particular who influenced me to become a teacher is Melva Price. She was one of the first black high school teachers in our generation in New York. While I was at Wardleigh she came to teach. Although I never had her as a teacher, she was a wonderful person, and in more than one way she influenced my life. She had gone to Hunter College; not only was she a Hunter College graduate, she had been an outstanding student. She was Phi Beta Kappa before she graduated. All of the black students at Wardleigh would meet with her as a group, and we would talk about what was happening at school, what was happening in the community, and what was happening every place socially. She took us under her wing. Melva taught Latin at Wardleigh for quite a while and later at a high school in Staten Island until she retired many years later. [57] All of these experiences influenced me and I decided I was going to be a Latin teacher.

I taught at Wallkill for three years altogether, continued working there throughout my first year of marriage, then I joined my husband in Washington. After several years in the D.C. area, my husband took a job in the Midwest, running an antipoverty agency in Flint, Michigan. Flint was just beginning to expand its staff in teaching, and at the time, in the mid-fifties, the city was considered progressive because they were offering the same salary to men and women.

Flint was a big car manufacturing town, a company town. That was where all the Chevrolets were made and Buicks— Buicks and Chevrolets. Working in a car factory at that time was a good job and people earned a good living. There were a few white families still in Flint in the area where we lived, and their children came to the school where I taught. But I was the first black teacher in the Flint Public Schools. At first I had a hard time relating to the kids, and I think the problem was mutual. The families were mostly from Mississippi, and they felt that coming to Flint was a step up because before I came to teach, they had all white teachers. They had come out of Mississippi—where

---

[57] Besides being an influence on Ora, Melva Price influenced a number of other black women who attended Wardleigh High School during this same period. In her book, *Balm in Gilead: Journey of a Healer* (Reading, Mass.: Addison-Wesley, 1988), Sara Lawrence Lightfoot discusses the influence of Melva Price and other black teachers on the development and career of her mother, Margaret Lawrence.

schools were neglected, segregated, and staffed by black teachers. So it was easy to associate these terrible schooling conditions with black teachers. When I first came to the school neither the parents nor the kids were particularly pleased. I probably reminded them of what they had come to Flint to escape. In the beginning there was a lot of mistrust between the kids, the parents, and me. It took some time and a lot of effort to get to know each other, to work out the problems, and develop solid relationships. It helped that my children were growing up and attended the public schools in Flint.

I remember searching for ways to break the ice and form closer relationships with the children and their parents. The ice broke one day when I was wearing a pin of a beautiful African woman. As I talked with the children about the pin I learned that most of the children didn't think that the woman was attractive; she was very dark and had African features. That startled me because most of the children were very dark-skinned and also had African features. Their reaction to that pin bothered me. If they couldn't see the beauty in the woman, what did they think about themselves? I thought we should explore our common heritage—after all, I was only one generation away from the West Indies, and they only one generation away from Mississippi—by studying about Africa. As a result I developed an entire curriculum around Africa and the African diaspora. I brought in African artifacts from the West Indies and taught the children about the common ancestry of black people throughout the world. All of our subjects—geography, reading, history—revolved around Africa. What I was doing was creating a pan-African curriculum, but I didn't think about it in exactly that way. I was desperately trying to find a way to relate to the kids in order to teach them better. I was in Flint about twelve years, and in the end I had managed to develop deep relationships with the children and parents in that community. I still keep in touch with some of the children I taught in Flint.

There are lessons that I have learned from a long teaching career that are useful for teachers who are teaching today. A lot of things have changed, but a lot of things haven't. Isn't there an expression, "The more things change, the more they stay the same"? This isn't the first time ever that the schools are faced with children who have problems. When I was a child in New York, when I taught there during the Depression, and later in the forties, children had problems. Schools were overcrowded, children were poor, families were in distress, and immigrants were streaming into the country. It troubles me that people seem to have forgotten these facts. Sometimes I wonder what world these people were living in. Certainly not the same one I lived in. They talk about the past as if it were ideal, but believe me it wasn't. I don't know if we did a good job back then dealing with the problems. But if this society plans to continue, then all of us, and this includes schools and teachers, will have to face whatever problems there are and deal with them. We can't keep blaming someone else and passing the problems on to someone else. Today's problems belong to all of us.

Throughout my teaching career I have had to struggle to find ways to relate to the kids I taught because I didn't always feel I had a lot in common with them and I know the feeling was mutual. And they didn't think they had a lot in common with me. My whole experience teaching kids has been searching for and finding out what we had in common even when it didn't seem like we had anything in common on the surface. Today people are confused about how people are alike and not alike. A lot of people think that just because you are the same skin color as someone else you will automatically be able to relate to them, but what they overlook is the many ways people who look the same are different because of their different experiences. We are all more than our skin color, and just like we have to work at finding common ground with people who don't look like us, we may also have to find common ground with those who look like us but who may be different because they've had different experiences. Since your experiences influence how you see the world they can't be dismissed, brushed aside, or ignored. This is a critical lesson for today's teachers to learn. I've worked hard to find out what I had in common with the kids I taught, whether they were the girls in Wallkill, the pupils in Flint, or the junior high school students in Berkeley.

Over the years a lot of people tried to persuade me to move from the classroom to doing higher-level administrative work in the system. I always felt that the classroom was where I belonged, so I never succumbed. Some women did succumb to the lure of higher pay, but I didn't and I am glad that I stayed in the classroom. When I look back at the experiences I've had in my life, I realize that I was actually living out history.

RUBY MIDDLETON
FORSYTHE

In Charleston, South Carolina, in 1905, Ruby Middleton Forsythe was born into a family that by turn-of-the-century standards was middle class. We spoke in 1988 and again in 1989 in the one-room schoolhouse in Pawley's Island where she taught for almost sixty years, At the time of the interview, she resided in a small apartment above the schoolroom. Pawley's Island is a small community about fifty miles from Charleston and thirty miles from Myrtle Beach, a resort community on the South Carolina coast. Like other South Carolina coastal communities, the island has been affected by the recreation explosion, the equivalent of urban gentrification. As a result, black people have been displaced from their homes.

After attending a private school in the home of Miss Montgomery—a practice not uncommon among black middle class families at the time—Miss Ruby entered Avery Institute, a Charleston normal school for blacks founded by the American Missionary Society at the end of the Civil War. Unlike the Hampton-Tuskegee industrial model of education, Avery, like other schools sponsored by the American Missionary Association and other religious organizations, emphasized a more classical education.

After completing and receiving her licentiate of instruction from Avery in 1921, Miss Ruby began teaching in St. Pleasant, South Carolina. Between 1924 and 1938 she worked in the Charleston County schools. In 1938 she began teaching at Holy Cross Faith Memorial School until her retirement in 1991. In the 1950s Miss Ruby enrolled in South Carolina State University where she received a bachelor's degree in education. In 1989, Miss Ruby was featured in I Dream a World, *a book about influential black women who are commonly overlooked in history books.*[58] *Her portrait from this book was later used on a Children's Defense League poster.*

Told with a lilting Charlestonian accent characteristic of those from the Carolina Low Country, her narrative provides a glimpse into the experiences of those who lived in, were educated in, and taught in black communities during the early part of this century. Miss Ruby died on May 29, 1992, in Mount Pleasant, South Carolina.

My name is Ruby Middleton Forsthye, but everyone here calls me Miss Ruby.[59] I'm originally from Charleston, born and raised in Charleston in nineteen hundred and five, right at home, no hospital, born right at home. My house used to be on Chestnut Street on the west side. They changed the street; now it's Higgard Avenue. The section that we stayed in was known as Gadsden Green, or Fiddler's Green.

My father was a brick mason. In that time they did all the molding on the old houses. As a child, I would see him make these things made out of plaster for those old houses in Charleston, the decorations all around the ceiling and the baseboard. They don't do that now, so you don't see it on the new houses. My mother did domestic work, washing and ironing, but at home. She did the nurses' and doctors' uniforms.

I've been teaching for over sixty years. I've been on Pawley's Island fifty-two years, right here in this school. It's called Holy

---

[58] Brian Lanker. *I Dream a World: Portraits of Black Women Who Changed America* (New York: Stewart, Tabori and Chang, 1989).

[59] In the coastal communities of South Carolina, it is customary as a sign of respect to call older men and women Mister and Miss followed by their given names.

Cross Faith Memorial School, but most people around here call it Miss Ruby's School. Before that I spent fifteen years teaching in Charleston. I've seen a lot of things in this time. Ever since I've been teaching and even before I began teaching, it's been hard for black teachers and pupils. When I began school it was in a private school with a teacher named Miss Montgomery. I stayed in Miss Montgomery's school until I finished sixth grade. I got all my lower training right there in that private school. There were not many students in the first school. It was more of a family group. It wasn't in a school building. Miss Montgomery taught right in her home. When I was young a lot of private home schools like Miss Montgomery's were started by Avery students because their parents didn't want them to go out into the county to teach.[60] By opening up home schools, black teachers were able to support themselves and some black children got to go to decent schools. There were quite a few private schools like Miss Montgomery's in Charleston back then.[61] There wasn't any integration in Charleston at that time; black teachers had to go out into the county because Charleston didn't hire black teachers to teach in the public schools. Everything was white until around 1917 when Septima Clark, along with the principal, and the students at Avery organized to get black teachers into the Charleston city schools. I was a student at Avery when they organized a petition and went door to door collecting signatures in the black community so that black teachers could work in Charleston. That made a lasting impression on me. It convinced me that things can change when black people organize.

My mother planned and saved for me to go to Miss Montgomery's school. I was a bit obstinate, and she knew that these white teachers weren't gonna be able to tell me, "You do so and so, you got to do so and so," and I would just do it. She thought that having white teachers treat black children like that was too

---

[60] *Initiative Paternalism and Race Relations: Charleston's Avery Normal Institute*, Edmund L. Drago (Athens: University of Georgia Press, 1983) also describes the Charleston practice of Avery graduates opening home schools.

[61] In the book *Lemon Swamp*, Mamie Fields discusses a school she attended that was organized and taught by her cousin, Miss Izzard. Annie Izzard was a graduate of Avery Institute.

much like slavery. So Momma felt like she had to sacrifice and send me to Miss Montgomery.

After that I went to Avery Institute, a school run by the American Missionary Association. I started there in the seventh grade and stayed until I finished the senior high school. Avery had a two-year teacher training course. When you finished that, you got what we call an LI degree, a Licensed Instructor. At Avery we had a classical education, not the vocational education that some of the other schools were passing off on our black teachers. I was trained to work with the little children because the teachers at Avery felt that's where my talent was. I left there and I went to work in Charleston County.

By the time my sister graduated from Burke High School, things had changed in Charleston and she was able to get a job teaching in the public schools. But, even after she got hired, black teachers still had a hard time. If they were too political, they could lose their jobs. My sister always belonged to the NAACP, but she never let anyone know because she was afraid to lose her job. One of the big showdowns we had in Charleston came around 1945; that was the Smith Case. This teacher had signed on her application blank that she was a member of the NAACP, and the school system dismissed her. That's when they called those NAACP lawyers. Everybody went to court to see how that case was going to turn out. Those black lawyers argued that case. They sat there and they would just tell them the number of the page and what the law was. They knew what they were doing. Those black men had those white boys shaking. They had those white men stung. Those NAACP lawyers, that was one group whites respected. The Smith Case was one of the first cases dealing with discrimination against black teachers that we had in Charleston.[62]

---

[62] Probably refers to the case that dealt with pay equalization for black teachers. In the mid-1940s black teachers in Charleston and Columbia, South Carolina sought the same pay as white teachers. A case requiring the equalization of salaries had been ruled upon in Virginia in 1940 and upheld by the United States Supreme Court in 1941. When black teachers asked the South Carolina legislature to appropriate the money for their salaries the legislature refused. Richard Kluger, *Simple Justice* (New York: Vintage, 1975), p.16.

I've been on Pawley's Island fifty years in this same school. I came here in 1937 and started working in the school with my husband, William Esseck Forsythe, in 1938. I got married in twenty-eight but stayed in Charleston while he was in Pawley's Island until thirty-seven because I had to take care of my mama and daddy who were up in age and needed me. I wouldn't leave them because I felt that they had done a lot for me and I should be able to do for them, then. If my husband wanted me, and if he wanted that arrangement, then that was fine. If he didn't want that, then he had to go on about his business. He must have been satisfied with the arrangement because we were married about forty-seven years when he died.

My husband was part West Indian. His father was a South Carolinian from Orangeburg, but his mother was West Indian. He came to Charleston from Florida to work under the Archdeacon at Calvary Episcopal Church, which was my church. That's where I met him. He stayed in Charleston from 1925 until they sent him over here, to take charge of the work at Pawley's Island, so that's how I got here. He was the priest in charge of the little church and then he ran the school. At that time church and the schools were together.

We had one son, Burns Maynard, named after the two grandfathers, Burnes and Maynard. That's all, I wasn't gonna have no more. For a while I had him with me in Charleston. Later I brought him and he stayed here about two years. He went to school, and then I sent him back to my sister in Charleston, to go to Avery.

He was in one of the last classes to graduate from Avery. From the beginning, the city never did like having a black private high school. Now, you may wonder why Charleston didn't like Avery. It was the cultural part. They could see that the cultural part—that made a difference in the children—in their education. In the public school for blacks they stressed washing, ironing, farming, and cooking—domestic sciences, they called it. What they wanted were black housekeepers. "Scrub those floors and learn how to cook." The academic part in the public schools was not stressed as much as the academic part down at Avery. And the white community didn't want blacks to be educated out of their place. Eventually the city managed to get involved in Avery because Avery accepted money from the city. Once that happened, the school was doomed. It stayed open two more years, and after that it was closed.

Before coming to Pawley's Island, I taught in Charleston County. I stayed in the county for about fourteen years, from 1924 to 1938, moving around to different schools. I lived with a family out in the community during the week and went back to Charleston on the weekends. In those small communities, I taught all grades, first through eighth. In addition to all of the school subjects, I taught sewing, handicrafts, art, and crochet. Every year we'd plant a garden. I always enjoyed working in the rurals, with the Little People.

White missionaries started Pawley Island's Holy Faith Memorial School in 1903. They started it for the benefit of the children who lived and worked on the rice plantations in the area. At the time there wasn't a public school for black children, not until later on. Once the public schools opened, they weren't fulltime. They only went for six months, but this school went for nine. When I first came here, there were about five teachers. The school went through tenth grade. In order to attend high school, the children had to travel to Georgetown. Our children only spent one year in public schools in Georgetown because the public high schools only had eleven grades back then. It wasn't until later on that twelfth grade was added to the public schools.[65] The children learned Latin, algebra, and everything before they left here.

When I first came here, in 1938, it was awful. I stood on that back porch and cried for one solid month. At that time you couldn't see anything but trees, woods, and there were no electric lights. We used wood-burning stoves to warm the building. I came from the city, and this was the country.

---

[65] It was common for school districts in South Carolina to end at tenth or eleventh grade. Between 1940 and 1958 school districts in South Carolina underwent tremendous changes. Teachers were required to have certification in order to teach, expenditures increased, school buses were provided for black school children and the curriculum was expanded to include twelfth grade. For a discussion of this, see Ernest M. Lander, Jr. *A History of South Carolina, 1856–1960* (Chapel Hill: University of North Carolina Press, 1960), p.229.

Keeping the school open hasn't been easy. The first problem was when the county decided to build a highway. In order to build the road, they cut through our property. All this property used to be closed in. Now the church cemetery is across the street. Part of the land where the state wanted to build the highway went straight through our property so we had to move the school. At one time two-thirds of the property on this island used to be black people's land. When the county wanted to build a bridge and a highway, they took our land and they took the land of black folks. They just took what they wanted. They condemned it and what they didn't condemn they took.

I know one fella had twenty-eight acres, and they gave him $2,000. The state had to pay the diocese a fair price for cutting through their land, but they didn't have to pay black people. That's the difference between how the state treated the diocese and how they treated blacks. They took his land back then, and they still are taking it today. There's a woman who has some land near here and they keep wanting to buy it. But she doesn't want to sell it. So they just raise the taxes. They know that poor black folks don't have the money to pay. I tell people, "Join the NAACP." Understand? And I say, "They will help you if you help them." But so many of them, on account of their jobs believe that if they belong to the NAACP, they'll lose their jobs. So there's no justice yet.

When I first came here, I had the first grade. Gradually, the teachers left until I had first, second, third, and fourth grade, another teacher had fifth, sixth, and one had the seventh and eighth. We worked like that, side by side, until 1950. Then we had the next fight. The county had built a new school. They wanted us to close this school and all of us to go together to the new school that they built. I told them I didn't want to leave this school to go to the new one. I didn't trust them because I know how badly they treated black teachers. One of the teachers from our school went over to work in the new school. When she went over there, they promised to keep her for three more years, but they only kept her two. One year they just put her out. That was it. And that cut her out of getting her retirement.

The next year the diocese said that they couldn't support the school, but if we wanted to keep it open we could do it. Then we had more trouble. The minister of the church in Georgetown stirred the parents up, telling them that if their children came here to school that when they finished here they couldn't go into the public schools for a higher education. Then the county wouldn't let us continue paying into the teachers' retirement fund. What we had in there we had to draw out. They said that they were going to see that this school closed. My husband told them, "We'll see that it stays open." And that's when we started the ball rolling. That was the beginning of the argument between the superintendent and us.

We got the Department of Education in Columbia hopping. We kept on going, but some of the parents pulled their children out; you know how the authorities can frighten some parents off. Then when they built the junior high over here at Wacamaw, that took the seventh and eighth grades from our school. They did everything they could to make us close the school.

Finally the diocese said if we wanted to keep it and the community wanted it, we could keep it open and that's what we've been doing ever since. We do it without much support. The diocese gives us $62.50 a month each year. The rest comes from other donations and activities that the parents sponsor. The diocese still wants to close the school. They've been hounding me, asking me, don't I think I want to rest? Don't I feel like it's time to retire? I told them last year that I have a class I want to finish up this year, that after this year maybe I'll make a decision. They feel that it's time for me to come out of the classroom. They would be happy if the school closed tomorrow—the state, the county, and the diocese.

You always hear people talking about how black folks should do more for ourselves. White people have always made it difficult for us whenever we have done something for ourselves. They want to be involved, telling us what to do and how to go about it. White people always feel that they know what's best for black folks; and they always have to be in charge. But regardless of what white people think about this school, the community thinks the school serves a good purpose. The parents don't want me to close the school. That's the reason we get the support we do.

During the time I've been here, thousands of children have gone through this school. I have taught three generations of families. I've taught their grandmothers. I've taught their mothers and now I am teaching their children. I have children here from ages three to ten. A lot of people wonder how I manage. But this school is run like Miss Montgomery's, the one I went to as a child. It's like a family.

The first thing I do is I try to become a mother to all of them. I let them know I care about them. I tell them, "As long as you are here with me, I'm your mama until you go back home, and when you go back home, you go to your other mother." Once you get the affection of those little ones, you won't want to teach any other group. You have to be tender but firm and positive. So you show them that motherly affection. It's only after you've established some affection that you can talk about discipline. I do not get all caught up with this liberal-conservative argument about what's wrong with our children and what's best for them. As far as I am concerned, right-wing, left-wing, no-wing, everybody needs discipline. You can't accomplish anything without discipline.

There's a little boy in my school who used to attend public school before coming to me. He was only in the first grade, but whenever he misbehaved, they sent him home. Now, what do little children in the first grade care about going home? They are going home to play. Instead of taking the time to correct black children or discipline them, the teachers send them home or else they suspend them. I don't send children home. I work with the children and their parents until their behavior changes. It is impossible to discipline or teach black children unless the children believe you care about them. You've got to care, and you've got to be positive and determined.

This school opens early in the morning. The children arrive between 7:30 and 9:00 A.M. Many of their daddies drop them off on the way to work. Others come to school in individual buses that carry people to work in the hotels and resorts on Myrtle Beach. So I open the school early to accommodate them. The children come from all the neighboring communities. Some come from a place called Graves Station outside of Georgetown; others from Burgess, that's higher up. I've got some from Murrells Inlet, some from Sandy Island. Those from Sandy Island come across on the boat because there's no bridge. Then there are children who come from Georgetown proper. They come from all around. The parents start picking them up around 3:30 on the way home from work. I keep the school open until all of the children have been picked up.

My children start to read at four as soon as they learn their alphabet. You will hear a lot of experts say that you must not teach the alphabet as alphabets. I don't care what the experts say, each teacher has to find her own way to teach the children she has. Some of the methods that the experts tell you to use don't work with the group you have. So, I don't pay attention to what the experts have to say. I teach the children to recognize the letters as letters and in words.[64] I don't care what you get in college. When you come out and get in the classroom, you have to find your own ways to make sure that you reach the children you have in your classroom. It's up to you to find methods that work.

Some of the children come to me from the public schools usually after the schools are getting ready to put them in special education classes. Most of the parents don't feel that their children belong in special education classes, so they ask me if I will take them. These children don't need to be in special education. The schools and the teachers don't know how to work with these children. If I had them from three years old, instead of their parents sending them to day care and then into the public school, they would be much farther ahead.

There's a big difference between the children who come to me at three and those who come at seven. When children start

---

[64] For research that discusses the positive influence that learning the alphabet has on early reading, see Marilyn Jager Adams, *Beginning to Read: Thinking and Learning About Print* (Cambridge, Mass.: MIT Press, 1990).

here, regardless of how small they are, they're going to be in the Thanksgiving program, they're going to be in the Christmas program, they're going to be in the Easter program, they're going to be in the commencement program. I start them learning a recitation at the age of three. I put them in a little group and give them a piece to learn. Their parents practice with them until they memorize those pieces, and they perform them for the entire school. Some people don't believe that these three-year-olds can get up there and recite four to eight lines, but they do. Facing an audience, giving a recitation, and hearing that applause builds up their confidence and I keep building on that all the time they are with me.

In most black churches it's customary to have little plays with all the children in the congregation participating — even the tiniest ones — to mark religious holidays. At Avery every year we put on Shakespearean plays. I carried the idea to Charleston when I began teaching there. We always had an operetta at commencement and other plays to mark the religious holidays. The whole community turned out. I brought the idea right on to Pawley's Island, and I've been doing it ever since.

Getting an education has always been hard for black people. Now that the schools are integrated, getting an education is supposed to be easier, but it is still hard for black children to get a decent education. The obstacles are different than the ones we faced, but they still exist. Let me give you an example. Not too long ago, they had a science fair at Wacamaw. Out of all the black children—and some of them had good projects—not one of them got anything. Fourteen ribbons were given and all the fourteen went to the whites. Some of the black children said, "You mean to tell me that with all those good projects we had, no black got a prize?" Those children just spoke out, said what they felt, and they were suspended because they're not suppose to express themselves even when they believe that what is going on in school is unfair. That just kills their spirit.

When the children were integrated into white schools, they lost something. Integration has helped in some ways, but it has hurt our black children in some ways. Now, instead of seeing black children winning prizes for their achievements, you see them all in special education classes. This has caused them to lose their pride, their self-esteem. They have been pushed back, as far as leadership is concerned. Instead of being taught to lead, they are being taught to follow. So we shouldn't be surprised now that when one gets up and does something, then the whole bunch jump up and follow. Before, I think the older children were a bit more individual. They had a mind of their own. They couldn't be so easily led. And when they reached a certain grade, they had a sense of pride or dignity that caused them to act different.

Just like integration has hurt black children, it has also caused many of our black teachers not to be sure of who they are and what they are supposed to stand for. In earlier times most of our black teachers had a sense of purpose and dignity that they tried to instill into students. Some of our black teachers today are very concerned about our children. But we have too many who will tell the child, "I've got mine. You'd better get yours—because I know I'll get my paycheck." The black community doesn't need that teacher.

We have some white teachers—a few—who are concerned about the development of black students as well as the whites. But most white teachers fear that if that black child uses his ability he might override the white. There's a fear that black people are going to be successful, that if they do give a black child a chance that child will surpass this white child over there. There's a fear within the white group; deep down inside, whites fear that blacks might surpass them. They know that blacks have the ability, the potentialities are there. But they rarely give black children a chance and they don't really encourage them.

Many of the children from our school have a hard time when they go over to public school. The students and teachers don't like them, because they say they behave differently. That's because they don't play around, they take learning seriously, and they expect to be leaders, not just followers. For the most part, black children are not encouraged to do well by the public schools, so when our children leave here they are going against the grain. In spite of all the obstacles that they face, many of them do pretty well once they leave here. A lot of them are able to earn A's and B's. I get to see their marks because they bring them to me. If they make A's and B's, I give them something, put a little piece of money in an envelope and send it to them, just to keep their spirit up.

There's always been a lot of prejudice against black people. Today there is still a lot of prejudice and racism, and it's gonna be here for a long time. It won't be gone in my lifetime and not in these children's lifetime. I try to teach my children that they can't let that get in the way. We have to forget about those who try to keep us down, we have to protect ourselves, and we have to keep on going.

I tell the children that they have to push and struggle for what they want: "Don't go to school every day and just play until it's time to go back home, and be satisfied with that. When you enter that classroom, tell yourself you are there to get everything that you can because you're going to need it later." I also remind them that they have a responsibility to use their talent to benefit someone other than themselves, and that they have a responsibility to give something back to the community. I urge them to develop their talent so they can be of service to others; to become the kind of leaders that will enable others to gain something from them. I keep pushing that message on them. If I can just get the children to feel that they want to be somebody, that they want to do something, that they want to get somewhere, that they should help others, and that they should lead sometimes, not always follow, then I have accomplished my goal.

These are the lessons and the values I learned from my family, community, and school. And these are the same values and lessons I try to instill in my children. This knowledge is the gift I received from my community, a gift I've passed on to three generations, and as long as I'm able I'm going to keep on passing that gift on to these children.

MADGE SCOTT

*Born in Jacksonville in the 1920s Madge Scott received all
her schooling in Florida. She taught in segregated schools in
Jacksonville for four years before moving to Connecticut. A
widow, she retired from the Hartford public schools in 1983.
The interview took place at her home in Bloomfield, Connecticut. Her husband's artwork—pastel and charcoal draw-
ings, oil paintings, and sculpture—adorn her living room.*

Jacksonville was a small, sleepy Southern black town, a community where most people knew each other. The restrictions of segregation forced us together, and out of that we tried to make community. In school I was surrounded by teachers, all black, who
inspired me to go forth and try to do something in the community.
In Florida, at that time, teaching was one of the professions of
choice. For women it was teaching and social work. Women
worked in the school system; men worked in the post office. This
is where middle-class black people worked and these were considered good, steady jobs at the time.

At Florida A&M, I was supervised by a Jeanes teacher.[65]

---

[65] In 1907 Anna Jeanes, a Quaker, donated money that led to the establishment of
the Negro Rural School Fund. This fund supported hundreds of Jeanes teachers
who were charged with assisting the supervising county teachers. By 1936, 426
Jeanes teachers were employed in fourteen Southern states. By standards of the
time, Jeanes teachers were well educated; 46 percent of Jeanes teachers had
bachelor's degrees.

When I graduated from college, I went back to teach in the same school that I had attended as a child. James Green was a science teacher when I was in high school. When I began teaching, he had become the principal of the school where I taught. Two of my classmates and I worked alongside some of the same teachers who had taught us. They retired a few years after we began teaching, but they were still there when we started. We patterned our life, our teaching lives, after them. They welcomed us into their community of teachers. There was one teacher there who was ten years my senior, and she put her arms around me when I first started teaching and tried to help me out whenever she could. Her name was Cally Simpson. She was a good teacher and role model, and I learned a lot about teaching from her. This practice of young teachers coming back to teach in the school where they had once been pupils was not unusual and it was one way the community maintained a kind of continuity.

Even though the schools were segregated, the teachers did quite a few things with the curriculum that did not coincide with the white school and were not sanctioned by the school board. The teachers taught us a lot about our own race even though the school board prescribed a curriculum that didn't include any-thing much about black people. We sang the Negro National Anthem, "Lift Every Voice and Sing," before every class and assembly. All of the teachers knew that the supervisor or superin-tendent only came around every five or six months and when they came everything had to be exactly so. Any information we were learning about black people would be set aside and all the teachers made sure we were working on the official curriculum. When people think about black teachers, they don't see them as subversive, but these teachers were. Because they wanted us to know about our own race, they taught us things about ourselves that weren't in the books.

I taught English and social studies in Jacksonville, but when I came to Hartford, Connecticut, in 1947 they weren't hiring black teachers in secondary school. If you were black it was almost impossible to get a job at the secondary level, so I took a course in elementary education. While I was doing that I was a social worker for one year. I taught at two schools in Hartford, the Bonnet Brown School for sixteen years and the Mark Twain School until I retired in 1983. Both schools were mixed when I began teaching and by the time I left there were no white students left. Bonnet Brown was one of the oldest schools in Hartford. When I began teaching there were Italian children, children from the Ukraine, and everywhere else. By the time I left, the school was two-thirds black and one-third Puerto Rican. Now that school is almost entirely Puerto Rican. By the time I left Mark Twain School in 1983, there was only one white child in my class. As the neighborhoods changed so did the schools and now most of the schools in Hartford are predominantly black and Puerto Rican.

The differences between the schools in Jacksonville and the schools in Hartford were tremendous. Some of the differences had to do with me, but others had to do with the school system itself. One difference was that in Jacksonville all of the children and the teachers were black. Having grown up in all-black neighborhoods, I hadn't had much experience with whites, so I felt a little more comfortable around blacks than I did around whites. I wasn't comfortable with whites until I got to know them, because I had lived in an all-black world for twenty-four years. Going from teaching all black children to teaching a mixed group of children was quite a challenge. In the beginning, I wondered whether I was supposed to do the same things with these other children that I had done with black children, but after a while I found out that children are the same. After learning the ropes and learning what was expected of me, I became more comfortable in Connecticut.

There were other differences that took some getting used to. We didn't have as many materials in Florida as we had in Hartford. We had to make up our own lessons. Another thing was the school system in Hartford seemed to be far more relaxed than in the South. Everything in Jacksonville was very businesslike. There were certain things teachers were expected to do. I wasn't accustomed to walking into class just a minute before the children arrived and then leaving to go home as soon as the bell rang, but that's what I found when I arrived in Hartford. In

Florida we had to be at school much earlier than the children. The principal assigned each teacher different tasks to complete in the morning before school began and the same thing in the afternoons. We were expected to be around after school to work with children who needed extra help. So the teachers didn't rush out of school with the children. We stayed in our classrooms, did a whole lot of things after school: correcting papers, planning for the next day.

The principal in Florida was very strict. He was always in the classroom to see if you were doing what you were supposed to do. He would come into your class without telling you and sit in the back and sometimes stayed for an hour. The teachers accepted that as his right. I thought it was supposed to make me a better teacher. In Hartford the principal would come by the door and call you out of the class, but he never just dropped by your classroom unannounced to watch you teach. Teachers had locks on the doors, and I was surprised to learn that some of the teachers would go in the classroom and close the doors and they would lock themselves in with the children. That would never happen in Jacksonville. The doors were always open.

The discipline was far different from what it is now. I didn't agree with some of the things that happened. If children did not learn, if they missed a word that they were supposed to spell when I was coming along and when I first began teaching, they would get strapped on the hand. That was the disciplinary approach that they used in those days, but I didn't go along with that. Talking back or talking out was just not what we did in Florida. I disagreed with children not being able to say what was on their mind because I've always believed that children should have freedom of speech. But I also wanted the children to know where the authority began and where it ended. I always tried to teach them that along with rights went responsibilities. I told the children, "I'll always listen to you if you have something to say."

Another big difference between Jacksonville and Hartford came from the way the union dealt with the community. In Florida I belonged to the American Teachers Association, an all-black state-wide association. In Hartford the unions were not segregated like they were in Florida. I belonged to two different associations, the Connecticut Education Association and the Hartford Federation of Teachers. The Hartford Federation of Teachers was the local association that was affiliated with the American Federation of Teachers. They were not too popular especially with many black teachers, because they felt that the union would go along with the labor strikes and support teachers' interests over those of the black community. Remember, it was the American Federation of Teachers union that went against the community in the Ocean Hill–Brownsville incident.[66] A lot of the white teachers felt that the unions represented their interests, so they were eager to be in them.

I supported the union, because they were the ones who got the ball rolling as far as salaries and benefits were concerned. They had two or three strikes while I was in Hartford. Before they were about to go out on strike, I made it clear that although I supported the demands I was not going to strike. Nor would I cross the union picket line. What I would do was go to school before the picket lines started and stay until after they had left. I respected them, but personally, I didn't feel that as a teacher I should strike. The school had to stay open. Striking meant that black children who were desperately in need of schooling were going to be denied the opportunity to learn, and so I continued to teach.

Today there is a lot of talk about problems that kids have in school, especially black kids. I don't want to romanticize the past, but today there's too much permissiveness, and permissive behavior, where *people* not only children are concerned. Chil-

---

[66] In the fall of 1968 the American Federation of Teachers called a strike. The seeds of the conflict were planted when the Ocean Hill–Brownsville area of Brooklyn began an experiment in community control. Blacks were convinced that community control would improve the education in the community because the community would be able to decide which methods, curriculum, and teachers would be most useful for educating black children. The conflict escalated when the Ocean Hill–Brownsville board dismissed several teachers. Black parents and community members clashed with the striking teachers.

dren reflect the society; they are a barometer for all that is right and all that is wrong in society.

Black kids are also haunted by and have to overcome all the negative portrayals of who they are. Recently, there was an opinion piece in the paper that supposedly dealt with how to improve test scores for inner-city children. They had this cartoon of kids walking around with all this hair on their heads, snapping their fingers, and moving their heads to the music with these boom boxes under their arms. The writer was suggesting that the only way to teach black kids—to get them to score better on tests—is to let them carry these huge boom boxes around. This is the way black kids are being portrayed in the newspaper. In the days that followed there were several letters on the editorial page. But most of them missed the point entirely. Only one of them, written by a black man who is the principal of Weaver High School, found anything wrong with the cartoon. He said that the cartoon was just one more way of being biased and showing prejudice.

We have lots of black kids today who are very capable of excelling in school. But in too many situations teachers say, "Well, you know, you can't expect this of children who come from certain areas." The result is that the curriculum is being watered down. If you have high expectations for children, they will try to meet those goals. My belief is that you would make a child work up to and beyond his ability. And I don't think a lot of teachers do that today. But if this is how black kids are being portrayed to the entire community by the media, then it is unlikely that anyone is going to encourage them to use their ability.

Bloomfield, the town where I live, used to have a reputation for having good schools. But as more blacks moved into the community, people changed their perception of it and its schools.[67] A lot of people believe that if black people move to a town, the town is automatically on the decline. So, gradually, more and more people pulled their children out of the schools and sent them to

---

[67] In 1971 *Look* magazine named Bloomfield an All-American City for promoting desegregation. Although the population of Bloomfield is 70 percent white, the school system is 75 percent minority.

private schools, not only white people but a lot of blacks too. Now the public schools are predominantly black. Paul Cooks, the superintendent of schools, was quoted as attributing many of the school system's problems to "bright flight." I have always believed that if I pay taxes in a town, I'm going see that my child is getting everything that he's supposed to be getting. And if he isn't, I'm going to do something about it, even if it means having all the teachers booted out of the school. If you're in the town, and you pay taxes, you can influence the schools, especially if you're a professional. The thing to do is stay, fight, and not let the schools get worse. Instead of staying, parents—black and white—flee. But, if you pull your kids out, that's like the rush on the bank: If folks withdraw their money, the bank folds. Once Bloomfield was voted an All-American City and people had a lot of pride. Now people from the other suburbs, which are almost all white, have been trying to tear down the town's reputation. But that's the mentality of the white man who always feels that the moment black people move in everything is going to fall apart.

LEROY LOVELACE

*I began my interview with Leroy Lovelace by reading the
following quote from Sylvester Monroe's* Brothers, *a book
about growing up in Chicago and attending the school that
served the neighboring projects in which Lovelace taught
until he retired in 1994:*

> *He developed a ferocious reputation around the school which
> precisely suited his purposes. He was neither big nor tough, not
> by the standards of the street, but his room was a clearing in
> the forest, a place of silence, order, hard work, and nearly per-
> fect attendance. Being liked no longer counted as much to
> him as being a teacher, whatever the cost in popularity. But it
> would hurt him sometimes. He could not let himself ease up. He
> couldn't and he didn't. He claimed to be regarded with dread
> in the corridors and the freshmen who pitched up in his room
> were the objects of upper class pity. "You got Lovelace? Sweet
> Jesus. Poor guy.*

For the most part, what Sylvester wrote is true. Naturally, it's a bit
exaggerated, from my point of view. But if what he means by the
quote is that I demanded the best of my students, then he is accu-
rate. When I began teaching I was so idealistic. Having gone to a
private high school and a private college, I brought those expectations to public school. But the public school in which I taught was a
different ball game altogether. I found that I had to make more
demands because the students were a bit more lackadaisical in

public school than they are in private school. In private school, and in many suburban high schools, students do what they are told, for the most part. Whereas in public school I found I had to make my expectations clear. By making demands—I don't mean abuse, but consistency—not wavering from what you expect from the moment classes begin in September until the moment school closed in June. Students expect that. They might fight against it, but basically, students expect that from teachers. So, if that's what Sylvester means by "being tough," I'm afraid he's right.

In my dealings with students I demanded respect. I was honest, determined, and I expected the best of them. But I demanded as much of myself, probably more than I did of my students. By nature I'm serious, concerned, and caring. My students have good potential, and I expected them to strive and achieve their maximum potential.

Several years ago after being featured in a *Newsweek* article about urban teachers, I was contacted by the National Endowment for the Humanities to participate as a faculty member in the National Humanities Faculty Program. For three years I taught in the Maine Summer Humanities Project. The students who participated in the program were supposed to be the top students from throughout the state of Maine. Each of us taught ten kids four hours a day. These were exceptionally bright kids academically, most of them wealthy, and well-educated. It was a fantastic teaching environment. But while I enjoyed teaching there, it taught me to appreciate Phillips even more, because I was able to get the same results with my students at Phillips that I was getting with these privileged students in Maine. Not in the beginning, but by the second semester my students at Phillips were just as interested, sitting around talking, discussing, and understanding texts. The second semester I always told my students was the semester I was supposed to enjoy. I devoted the first semester to students, but the second semester was mine and I didn't let them spoil it.

Most of the teachers in the National Humanities Faculty Program were college teachers. They all wondered how I could tolerate teaching high school, especially in urban Chicago. I told them that I probably enjoyed my teaching as much or even more than they did, though I probably worked harder than they did.

If you had walked into my class, you would have seen my students rushing to get to class on time. Once they got to class, you would have seen the students getting out their homework, preparing to discuss the assignment, while I was checking the attendance roll. You would have see them talking with each other, conferring about the assignment. When class began you would have seen them all involved in a heated discussion. Some of them got annoyed with me because I wouldn't give them the answer when they get stuck. And you would have noticed that everyone was involved.

My idea of teaching wasn't simply standing in front of a class and expounding on something forever. Part of my motivation was to get everyone involved. When class ended you would have seen me pushing them out the door so that they could get to their other classes. When you left my classroom you probably would have wondered whether or not the class was being conducted in an urban Chicago school, a school that served students from housing projects.

Phillip's students were perfectly capable, but you had to demand their best. Initially they might fight you, but once they discovered that you were as determined as they were, they appreciated the fact that you didn't give up on them. Everyone who was in my classroom was responsible for making the class work. As I used to tell my students, "I'm just another member of the class. If this class goes wrong, you're just as responsible as I am, because each individual is responsible for making this class work. Don't expect me to be the only one responsible for motivating this class." It took a while to get that sort of chemistry working, but it worked.

The one thing that black students don't need is teachers who let them get away with saying, "I can't do this. I can't do that"— teachers who feel sympathetic because the students are black, or they are from the inner city, teachers who let them get away with doing nothing. Teachers have to realize that black students—or all students, but I'm talking about black students now—are very clever, especially with white teachers. Too many black students have learned to play the game, to play on a teacher's sympathy in order to get away with doing nothing. Teachers have to demand from black urban students the same as they would demand from privileged white students, and they have to be consistent. Urban black students can do the work and in the hands of skilled teachers they *will* do it. They may have to work harder to achieve success. All students will con teachers if they let themselves be conned. But it's often easier for black students to con white teachers because the students know that the teachers will pity them, feel sorry for them, and make excuses that these students can't do this, can't do that, or that's there's a problem at home. If teachers aren't careful, every other student will excuse his failure to do his homework by saying he had a problem at home. I am not saying I never accepted a student's excuse, but I refused to accept every lame excuse they have because that's what they expected.

It particularly disturbs me when I see black teachers letting black students get away with doing nothing. Black teachers who do this tell themselves they are doing this sympathetically, but I don't accept that. I believe that black teachers are doing it because we've become middle class. Once black folks were poorer than Job's turkey and now that we have joined the white folks, we're talking about "They can't do it." You'd be surprised how many black teachers do that.

In the past, black teachers demanded more of their students and they didn't care whether there was anything in it for them personally. A lot of my black colleagues thought I was too hard on students. But the students I taught didn't think that, because for several years when the students had teacher recognition I got almost every award. The award I treasure most was the Teacher Who Demanded Most of Students.

White teachers tend to give up too easily on the kids. They take the kids' resistance as not wanting to learn. But as soon as the teachers stop pushing, the students say that teachers didn't care because if they had they would have kept on pushing them. The kids see it as some kind of a contest. Every day, when I went into the classroom, I knew I had to be up to the challenge. I never understood it, but I never gave up because I'm not a quitter. I loved teaching, I didn't mind hard work, and I had faith in my kids. There was no way I was going let a kid who hadn't lived as long as I'd been teaching run my life, run me out of the classroom. I had to be the winner. There wasn't a kid clever enough to upset my teaching. Teaching was my passion. I never was willing to let some kid take that away. I enjoyed the game too much.

Too many teachers give up too quickly. Teaching anywhere today is hard work. It's especially hard in the cities because there are so many forces out there fighting against you: gangs, drugs, and peers. But teachers just have to keep working at it. If not, then they will be forced to give up. I had too much pride in myself, too much pride in the profession to give up.

My experiences in Brewton, Alabama, could have extinguished my interest in learning, but they made me all the more determined to get an education. I began school in Brewton in the little public school in the farm community where my family lived. Before my father purchased his own home, we had to walk quite a distance to school. The bus would come and pick up the white kid who lived across the street from us. The bus would pass us on the way to pick him up, turn around, pass us again before taking him to the school. Even though my mother tried to explain why he could ride and we couldn't, as a child I never fully understood why. Despite the inconvenience, Mother faithfully insisted that we go to school every morning, whatever the weather—cold, rain, or sleet. On rainy days we would be soaked by the time we got to school because it took us an hour and a half to get there. The school was a one-room building. Actually it wasn't a school; it was a church with one teacher who taught everybody. We sat on uncomfortable wooden benches that our parents had made and we wrote in our laps. There were no desks or anything. One teacher had to deal with six grades, seven, eight, or nine students at each level. She had her job cut out for her, but she struggled through it and was demanding of each of us. At the time, I just thought this was the way it was supposed to be. We were educated as well as we could be under the circumstances. Some of us went to college and became teachers. She did a pretty good job.

Back then the public schools for blacks only went up to tenth grade. There was private school for blacks in Brewton, but most black kids didn't continue because their parents couldn't afford the tuition, so they just dropped out after tenth grade. I won a partial scholarship to attend the private school, but I had to work to earn the rest of the money.

One of the most distressing things happened when I was a teenager pressing clothes in a downtown dry cleaners to earn money for school. I remember sitting in the window of this cleaners during my lunch period, looking across the way, across the park that we couldn't even walk through, let alone sit in. Up on the hill was a big palatial home used for a library. I remember seeing the white kids go into the library with a handful of books and leave with a handful of books. Although I enjoyed reading, I didn't have anything to read during the summer, not even paperback books. Even though that was a long time ago, when I think about it, it leaves a bitter taste in my mouth.

I attended the private school, which was considered a good school for the time, from seventh through the twelfth grade there. When I got to college, though, I was operating under a handicap because I hadn't read that much. I had been taught the grammar basics, but we read very few books or novels. When I got to college, I couldn't write a decent essay because we didn't do that much writing. When I went to Hope College I wasn't prepared in terms of reading or writing. My fellow students were much better read, much better educated.

Hope College was a top-rated Midwestern college, educationally speaking, but it was rigid about its beliefs. The school conveyed the feeling that if you weren't a member of the Dutch Reformed Church you wouldn't make it to the Promised Land. There were only a few blacks there at the time—two Ethiopians, one from Nigeria, and two from my school—so our social life was a bit constrained.

When I left for Hope College, I had intended to study for the ministry largely because one of the teachers in high school thought I would make a good minister. But while I was at Hope, after vacillating between mathematics and biology, I decided to become an English teacher. After college I moved to Chicago. For three or four years before I began teaching I did some graduate work and had a part-time job working at the post office. I used that time to educate myself, to re-read many of the books that I didn't have time to study closely while I was in college.

I started teaching at Phillips in 1958 and I retired in 1994.

Phillips School is an urban high school that serves students from the Robert Taylor Homes, a Chicago housing project. As a school we were not successful. There were successful classrooms, successful teachers, and some successful students. But most of the students who grow up in the Robert Taylor Homes never make it out. One, two, or three out of ten will make it, not necessarily because they are smarter but because they get a break or because someone—often someone in their family—pushes them with every force available to them. There are all kinds of success stories around Phillips, but they're so isolated.

American society doesn't want to educate all of its children. You always hear parents who can afford to send their children to private school complaining about spending their tax money educating someone else's children. This country would rather spend money on prisons than on education. Education should be the number one priority, but it's not. Rather than stifle teachers, school administrators could urge or motivate in order to bring out teachers' talents. Teachers have many talents and if they could overcome the petty jealousies and work together for a common good, students would benefit. You can't depend on politicians or the school board to improve the quality of education. All of the politicians talk about improving education, but they don't want to spend any money.

In Chicago there are local school councils. The politicians in Illinois have thrown the responsibility back on the communities, on the parents, to make a change. In my school, there wasn't one person on the council who had the appropriate training to work effectively in the schools. The state was tired of that responsibility, tired of being blamed for the failure of Chicago's public schools. Their response was to throw the responsibility on the parents, so that when things don't improve, the politicians can avoid the blame by shifting it to parents. They told the parents that they could choose the curriculum and spend the money on whatever they wanted. But when it doesn't work, the politicians will say, "You can't blame us because you have the schools you wanted." The parents on the council weren't educated or given the necessary training to understand how schools run. The secretary resigned because she couldn't take notes. Our school council was in disarray.[68]

Chicago has abolished the school board and now the schools are being overseen by a three-person committee composed of one black woman and two whites. It wouldn't surprise me at all if they gradually get rid of all of the black principals and replaced them with white ones.

I believe that education is learning how to think critically. When a people can think critically, they can change things. They are less likely to be taken advantage of and more likely to be able to avoid the traps that others set for us. An uneducated people can be taken advantage of because of their ignorance or naiveté.

Black people have to convince others how important education is for all of us, how we are all part of that black umbilical cord. Too many black teachers—they don't necessarily do it consciously—are forgetting about our roots, about how we are connected. If we leave everybody else behind, if we don't make time for the so-called "underclass," if we fail to educate ourselves as a group, what's going to happen to us all? If I can't see how a child who lives in a housing project and I are of the same umbilical cord, and do not strive to make us even more connected and share a common destiny, then we're lost. We black people can't expect someone else to do this. We have to do it ourselves. Because whether we like it or not in other's people eyes, no matter how much education we have, we are the pariahs. So, the main things are what we do with ourselves, what we think about ourselves, and what we can teach our kids to think about themselves.

---

[68] On 2 December 1988 the Illinois State Legislature voted to adopt the Chicago School Reform Act. The goal of the Act was to restructure the Chicago Public Schools. Under this legislation local school councils consisting of parents, community representatives, and principals were elected. These councils would have three tasks: adopt a school improvement program; adopt a budget to implement the plan; decide whether to terminate the current principal and select a new one or retain the principal and sign the principal to a four-year performance-based contract. For a more complete description of the Chicago School Reform Act, see G. Alfred Hess, Jr. *Restructuring Urban Schools: A Chicago Perspective* (New York: Teachers College, 1995), pp. 33-42.

BERNADINE B. MORRIS

Widowed, petite and soft-spoken, Bernadine B. Morris retired in 1987. She was born in Richmond, Virginia, in 1924 and grew up in the Fulton area, a black neighborhood near the James River,[69] which was destroyed when it was redeveloped under the Nixon Administration. She attended Armstrong High, the only all-black high school in Richmond. In keeping with the custom of assigning black principals and teachers to all-black schools in the South, all the teachers and principals she encountered up until high school were black. This practice was breached at Armstrong, where the principal was W. W. Townsend, a white man. At the time of interview she was preparing to attend her fiftieth high school reunion and had recently received a copy of the graduation program, which included a picture of W. W. Townsend. Though no longer a salaried employee, she tutors black children in a program sponsored by her church.

I remember many of my teachers from my childhood. Sara Brown, my first grade, was excellent. She taught at the same school for several generations. She visited her pupils' homes, and she insisted that all the teachers in that school also go visit

---

[69] See Scott C. Davis, *The World of Patience Gromes: Making and Unmaking of a Black Community* (Lexington: University of Kentucky Press, 1988), for an account of the Fulton community in Richmond, Virginia.

[53]

homes. In those days it was customary for teachers to visit their students' homes on a regular basis.

Although as a child you think you know your teachers, you really don't. Several years ago I was reading the Sunday paper and came across a headline that said, "Laura Jackson, the Pioneer." She taught me English at Armstrong High School. The article mentioned that she came from a family of educators. It described how she applied to go to the University of Virginia to work on her master's degree but was denied admission. It also reported that she was one of the individuals who fought to make sure that the state of Virginia furnished tuition money to black students to go out of state. Until I read that article I knew Laura Johnston only as a teacher. I thought that it was ironic that I had a teacher who was a hero, one of those persons who fought against the injustices against the black community.

I attended Fayetteville State Teachers College; the school had a rigorous program. Its reputation was so good, its graduates were virtually guaranteed jobs when they graduated. When I finished I had four choices. I selected Warrenton in Warren County, because the school was located in the town. I lived in a "teacher-age," a house where nine other teachers boarded right across the street from the school. It was a delightful situation, largely because of the *esprit de corps* that we developed. We did social things together. The group also encouraged its members academically, to pursue further education. It is unlikely that I would have started my master's degree as soon as I did if I had not been thrown into an atmosphere where people were going back and forth getting their master's degrees.

Most of the people in Warrenton were rural people and very poor. A few of them owned their own farms, but most of them were tenant farmers. Teachers were expected to be upstanding citizens and participate in community events. We were supposed to be models for the community, and the rules for our behavior were spelled out. One of the things the principal told me when I went to the interview was that we were expected to stay in the community at least one Sunday a month to attend church. He also said that although he realized that I was young and probably wanted to have some nice times, he cautioned me about going to the local beer gardens and advised me to go over to the next county's.

In Warrenton, teachers were respected by children and their families. I remember several Christmases, even though the families didn't have money to go out and buy the teacher a gift, the children would come to school with gifts, something that their families had raised. If you'd go to the home, the parents would often invite you back to dinner. They would notify you if their children were involved in various church activities and invite you to come and see. After teaching in Warrenton for several years, I worked in Charlotte, which was a much larger community. I have some good memories of my early years as a teacher in Warrenton and Charlotte. The relationships between black teachers and parents and the support we used to enjoy aren't like they used to be. And as a result children—black children—are suffering.

In both North Carolina and Virginia I also got involved in teachers associations. We had our own black teachers associations. Black and white teachers held separate yearly conventions on the same weekend, usually in the fall. In North Carolina, black teachers met in Raleigh; in Virginia, we met in Richmond. The white teachers met in a downtown hotel. But because we couldn't go into the hotels, we would gather at Virginia Union University. There were sessions and workshops on various topics—how to work with slow children or how to work with advanced students—all the newest trends. Professors, principals, and master teachers lecture, present workshops, and conduct the sessions. Once, I remember going to our conference in Richmond with some teachers from Hampton. At that time, because hotels and restaurants were segregated, we had to eat where we could. My mother fixed a big dinner, and I carried two carloads of teachers down to my mother's house to eat. Some of the teachers stayed there, some stayed in hotels. They had a couple of black hotels. But most of the teachers stayed with friends or else went back home every day.

These associations were also political and were very active in fighting for equalized pay. The Virginia Teachers Association— this happened before I came here—had a big fight for equalized pay, because the white teachers made more money than black teachers. The test case was in Newport News. Many of the black teachers who stuck their necks out to go to court lost their jobs in Newport News, and the Black Teachers Association hired lawyers to represent them. Some of the teachers who were fired in Newport News got jobs in Gary, Indiana, where they made more money. Still, they had to pull up stakes and in some cases leave their families just because they fought for equal pay.

I was one of the first black teachers to go into the desegregated schools in Hampton. I say "desegregated" because busing at that time meant closing the schools in black neighborhoods and sending the black kids to the white areas. They closed all the black schools. Greenbriar School where I once worked is now a recreation center. Murrow Peak, a school that the black community fought to have built for twenty years, was closed even though it was fairly new. Then integration came. Now Murrow Peak is a police academy. These schools no longer exist because they were located in black neighborhoods. The idea was to get the schools out of black neighborhoods—and they did a good job of it.

Whites who were against desegregation used to say it was terrible that they had to bus black kids. I often wondered where all of these people who were against busing were in the thirties when they were busing me past a number of schools to get to high school in Richmond. They had one high school to serve all the black kids in Richmond, and I had to pass two white high schools on a streetcar, which my parents had to pay for, to ride the city streetcar to get to Armstrong High School in Richmond, Virginia. I passed Thomas Nelson and John Marshall, which were all white. Nobody cried about busing then. I wondered where all of those who were opposed to busing were when the State of Virginia bused me all the way from Virginia to New York to get a master's degree. Nobody screamed then. So I can't see that much wrong with busing. Busing is busing. It's basically just transportation. It's what happens once the children get there that really matters.

What upsets me is that whether it was under segregation or integration, black people seem to have to bear all of the burdens.

In one of the all-black schools where I taught whenever the temperature dropped down below thirty degrees or thirty-two degrees, we were cold. There were times when the principal had to move us from one side of the building and double up classes because it was so cold. How can you teach in a doubled-up situation? I remember the day my girlfriend, who had a daughter in the school, called me up to say that her daughter had complained about the cold. When I told her that we were often cold, my girlfriend took off from her job at NASA, and she and another parent, who worked at the Veteran's Administration, went to the school for a conference with the principal. They didn't get much satisfaction.

The first ten or eleven years that I taught in Hampton black students never got new books. Our schools got books that the white kids had had at least three years. We never got the state adoption books until a few years after that book had been adopted, and then they had gone on to some new books. I remember an incident at Union, the second school where I taught. The books were so worn out that a first-grade teacher spoke up at a faculty meeting. She complained to the principal. She told him, "These books are so old the state adoption period has been passed. They're so dirty I don't even want to touch them myself." The principal agreed with her. He told us to go through the old books and stack all of those that were not usable outside of our rooms. He told the janitor to take them down to the furnace room to be burned. Two or three days after we got those books down to the furnace room the superintendent came to visit. When he saw the books stacked in the furnace room, he asked what was wrong. When the principal told him that the books were to be burned, the superintendent said, "There's nothing wrong with these books. The children can still read them." It was just not ideal at all. The books, the facilities, and the equipment at both Greenbriar and Union were not comparable to those of the white schools at all.

When the school system desegregated, the black community still had to pay the price. Because the school system decided to close or demolish the black schools, black teachers were going to be relocated to other schools. The reason given for tearing down black schools was that they were run-down. But that wasn't the only reason. The Union School was built of better material than the integrated school I went to; I went the first year they opened it, when it was brand-new. Union had beautiful hardwood floors and solid oak doors. It needed renovation, a new furnace, an updated kitchen. The parents had been fighting for these renovations. Around that time, a white school in the city caught fire one Saturday night, and by Monday morning the superintendent announced the school was going to be replaced. In the meantime, he was telling black folks that they didn't have the money to do the renovations they were requesting. They decided they would tear the school down anyway.

I was one of the teachers chosen to go to the white schools during integration. Before that there had been token black kids attending white high schools. They started with high school, and had a doctor's daughter, a Hampton University official's son, and a few other kids who had professional parents. The school system wasn't moving very quickly, and they were being challenged in court. A principal recommended me to be one of the first black teachers to go into a white school. He was supposed to be doing me a favor, but sometimes I wonder. He told me that he wanted to recommend me to the superintendent because he thought I would adjust to being in an all-white situation. I told the principal that I just didn't want to go under that kind of pressure.

I went home and I cried. I cried so much that my husband who was trying to be supportive kept trying to console me. Finally he said, "If it's going to bother you this much, why don't you make an appointment with the superintendent?" I didn't get a chance to see the superintendent, because he called all of us who were going to be transferred to white schools down to his office. There were fifteen of us and not a single one of them in there as dark as I am, not one. That ought to tell you something. After this meeting, it took about two or three days to get an appointment. When I finally met with the superintendent, he asked me why I wanted to stay at Union. I told him I was comfortable and successful there. He told me that eventually everyone in that school was going to be moved, within two years the school would be closing and torn down.

That's how I ended up at Booker Elementary. It was a horrible experience. There were about half a dozen black teachers out of thirty-six. Up to this time I had black principals, all black principals. This principal was terrible, a real redneck. We knew he did not want us there. When we walked into school in the morning, he didn't even acknowledge us, never said good morning. There were two or three teachers there, white teachers, who would pass us in the hall, and do you think they'd say good morning? They didn't say anything. Several times I had students who were acting up in the cafeteria, doing childlike things. These teachers wanted to make a federal case of it. They would say something like, "He's still talking when I told him not to talk." Well, this is what children do. I would always intervene and tell the teachers that I would take care of the problem. I had to do this, otherwise the teachers would make a big case out of nothing and then the children would get into trouble, be suspended or expelled.

Several white teachers in that school retired rather than work with black children. If they didn't want to teach black kids then they ought to leave. One year, the very first day of teaching, somebody had hired a black teacher at the last minute, the day before the teachers were supposed to report for work. The teacher didn't know where the school was located; she got lost. She got to school late while we were still in a meeting. She came in quietly, and the principal looked up and saw her. "I told you that you were supposed to be here by nine o'clock," he said, in front of everybody. "If this is going to be your habit, maybe we ought to discuss your employment." I was so embarrassed and angry that I wanted to go under the table. It was terrible, and it didn't get any better. We had several incidents like that between the principal—unfair and unpleasant incidents—and teachers and students.

After a few years the principal and I had a showdown. He had paddled a black kid; the child went home and told his family; his grandparents came and demanded an apology. I didn't see the incident, but the principal called me into the office to tell me about it. He was trying to explain himself to me, to get me on his side. I told him that I knew lots of other cases where he'd hit black kids with a paddle, but I've never heard where he had hit a white kid with a paddle; they have discipline problems too. He backed down off me.

He said to me, "Do you think that I'm prejudiced?"

I said, "Yeah. Yes, I do. And if you polled every black teacher in this school, they're going to say the same thing. Now, I haven't talked to them, but they're going to tell you the same thing I told you. I think you're prejudiced."

And then I brought up some incidents. I mentioned the black teachers who'd left and told him that he hadn't supported them.

He went around and asked the other black teachers whether they thought he was prejudiced and they all told him he was. Eventually this principal got a lot of criticism from parents, black parents, about the way he treated black kids, and finally he got reassigned, but he had managed to do a lot of damage by then. Teaching in this desegregated school was not easy then, and it isn't easy today.

I think when they integrated the schools, instead of the black kids seeing themselves as people who could go in there and make progress, they got linked and then linked themselves to all the bad things that the kids were doing. I can only relate to when I was in a segregated school. You'd go to high school commencement and I could see these kids walking up there with these four-year scholarships to places like Fisk and Howard or A&T or wherever. Now when I go to a high school graduation, the only kids I see getting the scholarships are white kids. Even those who make it to college have problems.

For a while I was the adviser for the Alpha Kappa Alphas for Christopher Newport College in Newport News, and I could see these kids sitting down in the cafeteria, drinking beer or playing cards when they should have been in class. I asked them how they could sit there, drink beer, and not go to class. And when I did, they would go to class. But there was no one up there concerned enough to tell them that they should do otherwise. I was up there for eight years as an adviser to the sorority, and some of these kids never got out of basic courses. They weren't graduating and the college wasn't doing much about it because the students were still paying tuition. Of course, these are young people and they don't see that they are being exploited. Every once in a while, I see some of those same kids today working in fast-food places. I call them food engineers. Is that what we want for black kids? So the miseducation begins in the elementary school and continues right into college.

Black kids need teachers who can understand and appreciate something about black communities. Too many white teachers don't understand blacks and don't want to understand us, yet they expect us to be able to understand them. We shouldn't have any problems, because we ought to know how to deal with them. But they have problems because they don't know how to deal with blacks. Why is that? I've seen white teachers let black kids misbehave and then when I ask them why they say, "I thought that was a part of his culture." I say, "Listen, these children have to be taught what's right, what's acceptable, and what's not acceptable. I don't care what color they are. And what you saw them doing is not acceptable." These teachers just shrug their shoulders and go down the hall. It's a lack of understanding the culture and a lack of commitment. It's a lack of understanding that what's right and what's wrong is wrong for blacks as well as whites; an unwillingness to take risks and really get involved with black children. Don't make excuses for them and say, "I think this is what they have been accustomed to doing." If they have been accustomed to doing it and it's wrong, then you must start teaching them the right way to do it.

Throughout my career in the classroom, and even now as I work with children in the tutoring program at my church, I teach black children as if they could one day grow up and be my neighbors because they could and they did. But I don't think that most white teachers can ever imagine that the black kids they are teaching today will grow up to be their neighbors. If they could, they would know that they have to get involved with them and then they might find a way to teach them. It saddens me that so many of our black kids today are doing so poorly, even after integration. It saddens me that integration didn't turn out to be everything we had hoped for.

Part II

THE VETERANS

CHERYL THIGPEN

She is forty-nine, born and raised in Boston. Until fourth grade, Cheryl Thigpen lived in a predominantly black neighborhood in the South End of Boston.

During the summers of 1987 and 1988 she participated in a program that placed educators in industry. Her assignment: Xerox.

I grew up in Boston. Although we lived in a black neighborhood and the church we attended was all black, I can only remember knowing one black fireman and one black policeman. Even though all the children in the school I attended were black, there was only one black teacher that taught in my school. As a child, I never gave this much thought. It wasn't until much later that I realized what a racist city Boston was.

I went to undergraduate school at Hampton University, and then I went home to Boston to attend graduate school at Simmons College under a fellowship program in urban education. Although I had substitute taught in Boston, I didn't want to teach in the Boston schools because of the continuing uproar over desegregation. I wanted hassle-free teaching, so I picked Hartford, Connecticut. That was in 1969. Like a lot of urban areas at the time, Hartford was actively recruiting black teachers. The day I went to Hartford, I was interviewed and offered a contract; I signed it. My first job was as a second-grade teacher at the Clarence A. Barber on Powell Street. I stayed there only a year because my principal was leaving Barber School to go a brand new school that was opening in Hartford. It was an open-classroom school, the newest thing in education at that time.[70] The principal began talking to me about this school. He must have talked a real good story because he talked me into believing that I would like the new school. I went to visit a few schools in the area that were using the open education concept and was convinced that it would work. In April they collected the staff for the new school, we went to the University of Hartford to take some preparatory courses, and then that whole summer we attended a special summer school program.

This was the newest thing in education and I thought it would be great for black kids because it wouldn't be as restrictive as traditional classrooms. The school had multigraded classrooms. I thought this would be a great innovation because it would be more like family, where students could spend several years in the same classroom and they wouldn't have to spend the first few weeks of each school year sizing up and testing the teacher. I had real high expectations for the school. But as the year went on I gradually began to change my mind.

We taught in teams. In order to teach effectively in a situation like that you have really got to know your teammates. I worked with two people, one male and one female, whose philosophy of education was totally different than mine. Our philosophy about learning was the same, but their philosophy about the kids was entirely different. Their philosophy was: "If Johnny doesn't feel like reading today, we're not going to make Johnny read, because if we make Johnny do things, Johnny's not going to enjoy them, and Johnny won't learn from those things." My philosophy of education is: "Johnny's got one strike against him already because Johnny is black. So when he comes to school he is going

---

[70] Popular in the late sixties and early seventies, open classrooms sprang up across the United States. The elements of open classrooms included: flexible use of space and time; multi-age, multigrade classrooms; learning centers; student choice of activities; small-group instruction, self-directed rather than teacher-directed learning, and active rather than passive learning.

to read whether he wants to or not, because his mother has sent him to school to learn to read, and if he can't read he's going to have two strikes against him."

The two people on my team just let the kids do what they wanted, whenever they wanted to do it. They were too permissive. These children were only first-, second-, and third-graders, six, seven, and eight years old. Children need adult guidance to learn how to make appropriate choices. All of the black children chose gym, art, or music. The school was set up so they could do whatever they wanted to. I believed that we needed to make kids aware that there was also reading, math, and social studies. I have nothing against gym, music, and art; that's all part of the school curriculum. But the children have to incorporate academic subjects into their school schedule.

But the day that I really began to have serious reservations about the school system's intentions was the day when we tested the students. Our instructions were: These kids are going to come out on top, regardless of how it's done. What they were saying is that whatever you have to do to make these kids test well, whether you have to show the kids the answers, tell the kids the answers, or whatever then do it. This was a model school and, no matter what, it had to come out on top. Of course, when the article came out in the *New York Times*, our kids tested better than anybody. Before that I was going to give open education a second chance. But after the testing and the article in the *New York Times* came out, I knew then that I had to leave because I couldn't be a part of the educational malpractice being perpetrated on the black community, so I put in for a transfer.

By the time I requested a transfer, it was too late. But, like everything else in the school system, it was a matter of who you know. I went downtown, talked to someone I knew, told them what had happened, how I'd decided I wanted to leave because I was very discouraged with open education, and that I felt I needed to go back into a regular classroom. Three days later I received a telephone call telling me to come down to the board. The man told me he'd give me a transfer on one condition—that I agree to take a second-grade class at a particular school. He had a son going into second grade who couldn't read, and that's the class he wanted me to teach. I was reassigned to the Watson School as a second-grade teacher and stayed there about six years. Except for three years when I worked as a project consultant with a system-wide computer assisted math program, I've been in the classroom since 1969 teaching mostly black children.

Everyone is talking about the current crisis in urban schools. People were talking about a crisis in urban education back in the sixties when I first started teaching. Then, the solution was to recruit a new group of teachers. One of the ways they got teachers to go into urban schools was by offering forgivable education loans. If teachers worked in a validated school, a school in which a certain segment of the children were below the poverty level, they did not have to pay the loan back. A lot of teachers came into the urban schools under that program, not because they were interested in working with urban black children but because they did not have to pay their student loans back. That has created real problems. In cities like Hartford, where the makeup is predominantly minority kids—the school population is something like 82 percent minority—where can these teachers who don't want to teach black students go? There are a few schools that still have white kids, but everybody certainly can't teach in those schools. They're not going to the suburbs because the suburbs don't pay like the city. The salary in Hartford is much higher than in the suburbs. These teachers stayed, got their loans paid off, and now they are here against their will, they're just here because it's a job and they have nowhere else to go.

I was working with urban black kids because that's where I wanted to be. I have always felt that the knowledge I have should be shared with black kids. Why should I pass it out to little white kids? They're going to make it in this world. A lot of white folks out there, even if they don't learn how to read or write well, there are still opportunities for them. White folks are still going to give those white kids jobs. I've always felt that I was too talented and had too much to give to white children. Other friends of mine who have chosen to teach in white schools feel just the opposite. They believe that if black teachers don't go into white schools, then white kids will never know black people and that black people are capable of doing things. Those reasons are just as valid as mine, and I respect that view.

My perspectives were formed at Hampton, the historically black college where I went to undergraduate school. Hampton had a long tradition of training teachers, and the education program, while I was there, was outstanding. For one thing, the department chair told us that people look at elementary education as something reserved for those who can't do anything else, and she made it clear that she didn't want us in the program if we felt we couldn't do anything else. She emphasized that teaching was a profession. She made us responsible for organizing an inservice workshop for teachers throughout the region. We had to choose the topic, get the speakers, and make all of the arrangements. There was a lab school on campus that was attended by the children of the faculty where we tried out our lessons. I learned a lot at Hampton. It was at Hampton that I discovered that I really had a talent for working with children, where I formed my basic philosophy about teaching and learning, and where I first met black teachers who became my personal role models. They were not only excellent educators, but they were leaders on the campus and in the community who gave of themselves to black students.

In the twenty years I've been in education very little has changed as far as the schools are concerned. Twenty years ago urban education was popular. Now it's teaching at-risk and minority populations. It's the same problem, just a different label—special education, children with special needs, learning disabilities. The question is how we teach children who have difficulties learning.

There have been tremendous changes in society that affect schools. In the past few years I've seen a higher number of kids with learning difficulties. The parents are getting younger and younger. It's not unusual to see a six-year-old kid with a twenty-year-old mother. My own theory about this is that the mothers themselves aren't fully developed, and when they have children they aren't able to give them all they need. This has a lot to do with the increase in the number of children with learning problems.

The public tends to see all urban schools as having extreme problems. My school is located in a very stable neighborhood. We don't have a big transient population. Most of the students come from families where the parents own their home's; so our families are fairly stable. If anything, we have kids moving into the school.

Rarely do we have kids moving out of the area, and if they do they're moving out of the city. That makes a big difference in the kind of parent relationships I am able to develop and sustain. Often, I've older siblings in my classrooms. However, over my teaching career, I have noticed a decline in parent participation. I haven't seen a decline in parent interest, but there has been a definite change in the amount of time parents are directly involved in school activities. I attribute that to economic factors. In most families both parents have to work, and more and more parents have to hold down more than one job just to keep a roof over their families' heads.

Everybody expects the schools to deal with society's problems. Whether it's sex education, drug education, or AIDS, they want the school people to deal with the problems. What about the other institutions in society? Why not have doctors or nurses deal with these issues? Why does the teacher always have to be the expert on everything? Even though we are asked to take on all of society's problems, there's very little investment in education or the schools themselves.

The building I teach in is sixty years old and it hasn't been remodeled. All of the fixtures, the bathrooms, the furnace are the same as when the building was first built. The only new things are the furniture and the windows. There is a big difference between a building built in 1920 and one needed to meet the requirements of the 1980s. But teachers are expected to carry on our work in spite of these conditions.

In cities with large minority populations, where the social problems are even greater, there has been even less investment in education and schools. For years white people controlled the schools, and even in cities with large minority populations whites didn't want to give us these positions. By the time the schools were finally in the hands of black superintendents, administrators, and school boards, the schools were in such dire straits that it was almost impossible for them to be turned around. Everywhere you look, some minority school superintendent is having a problem. If the scores are declining, blame it on the black superintendent; if there's violence in the schools, blame it on the black superintendent. Very few people take into account that the schools have been under the leadership of whites for years, and that their leadership is partly responsible for the problems confronting schools today. Regardless of whether the kids are white or black, there are so many evil forces out there working against our kids these days that these forces can overwhelm a school. Drugs, health, economic, and social problems—they are all working against kids and creating havoc in poor, black communities. As soon as they appoint the black superintendent he's automatically responsible for solving all the problems whether he created them or not. Hartford hired a firm to manage its public schools and even they weren't able to turn the schools around.

My relationships with parents have always been good. I can only think of a few incidents that have been negative. I usually contact parents during the first two weeks of school. Kids are usually on their best behavior during the first two weeks, so there's nothing I could possibly say to a parent about their child that is negative. When I call I tell the parents that I am their child's teacher, that I give homework every night, and urge them to call me or send a note if they have questions, and also the times when they can find me at school. I tell them: "This is your classroom, feel free to come in."

During the summer I have held jobs other than teaching. In the summers of 1987 and 1988 I was one of thirty-four teachers selected in the state of Connecticut to work with the Connecticut Business Industry Association. For a number of years they have selected teachers to spend the summer working at a corporation. I was fortunate enough to be assigned to the marketing department at Xerox. The experience was fascinating, much different from being in the classroom. The first year I worked as a technical writer; I had to study a particular machine or product and write a manual to teach someone how to use the product.

My teaching skills were useful in the corporate environment. Essentially, I approached the task from the perspective of the learners, as if they did not know anything about that machine. It was my job to teach them about the machine. It was exactly like conceiving and carrying out a lesson. I was very confident in what I was doing, and I had no doubts that I could do it.

When I applied the second year Xerox told the council that

they would only be interested in participating in the program if they were able to get me back. That made me feel good. The second year I was assigned to the Customer Support Division. I went out on service, installation, and training calls with some of the other support personnel. It was Xerox's fiftieth year, and they had put out a whole new line of products that year. My main assignment was teaching customers how to use one new product that the company was promoting. What surprised me was how much it was like teaching my students. Some of the office people I trained were afraid of machines.

In some ways, working in a corporate office was a radical change from teaching school. Being able to leave the building, which teachers can't do, and having a leisurely hour-long lunch break instead of the twenty-six minutes I get when I teach are things that most working adults, but not teachers, take for granted. Those two summers were eye-opening experiences. From my perspective coming from the classroom, it seemed to me that the people were getting paid to do nothing. I was also disturbed by the waste. Someone would put paper in a machine and if the machine jammed they would take the whole ream of paper out and throw it away. The waste didn't even faze the employees. I spent those two summers collecting everything that they threw out to use in my classroom. When I compared the modern facilities of Xerox with the old, dilapidated school buildings in which most teachers have to work, or all the resources and supplies they possess with the difficulties we have getting essential supplies, I get angry.

The summers at Xerox made me realize how little society values children, especially black children. But my experience at Xerox convinced me how important the skills that I had perfected in my classroom were. At Xerox I encouraged people to take risks, used a variety of techniques to teach a concept, assessed what they knew and didn't; these are the same things I do in the classroom. I always tell my first-graders, "I'm the best first-grade teacher, and you're so lucky to be in my class." I used to think I was a good teacher. Working at Xerox made me *know* that I'm a good teacher, and made me realize how much I love my job; how much I love teaching.

ETHEL TANNER

Before becoming a teacher, Ethel Tanner worked briefly as a probation officer. She was born and spent half her childhood in Austin, Texas, before her family moved to Roxbury (Boston), Massachusetts. Compared to her close relationships and personal experiences with black teachers in Austin, her relationships with teachers—black or white—in Boston were nonexistent.

After marrying, she moved to California. She is president of the board of Samaritan House, a nonprofit social service agency on the California Peninsula. She attends churches of many denominations but prefers Glide Memorial Church in San Francisco because of its social activism and ministry to the dispossessed. "You'll see all kinds of people at Glide Memorial—black, white, yellow, poor, rich—all kinds. And this is what I think church should be."

I remember many of my teachers and other adults from my schools in Austin: the teacher who taught me to tap dance, the physical education teacher who spent a lot of time with us after school, and the teacher in my elementary school who produced plays several times a year. Even the principal's secretary influenced me because, in the fifth grade, she organized a little society for students who made good grades. It was like a little club. It was kind of nice. I don't remember the teachers I had in Roxbury like I remember the teachers I had in Austin.

I am and have always been rebellious. I always knew my own mind. I knew what I wanted and was willing to take chances. When I was in elementary school, I quit the Methodist Church, my family's church, and became a Catholic. I was the only person in my family who was Catholic. At first my parents' response was negative, but after a couple of years they decided that was really what I wanted and they didn't die. That's when I first learned that taking chances wasn't that risky. I've put that rebelliousness into turning this school around.

One day the superintendent of schools of San Mateo County came to me and said, "I want you to do something for me, Ethel, because I know you can do it."

And I said, "Well, James, what is that?"

He said, "I want you to go to North Shoreview. And I want you to do something with the curriculum there."

This school had the lowest test scores in the district. When I went to visit the school on the first occasion, I found a group of demoralized teachers.

As I walked through the school I saw that all of the glass windows had been painted so the kids couldn't see out. When I asked why, the answer was: to keep the kids from daydreaming. When I asked about the reading program I found out that each teacher taught whatever she liked; some taught Bank Street, some taught Lippincott.[71] Out in the middle of that yard were three burned-down buildings that stood there with wire around them. The intercom machine only worked in one direction; the principal could talk to the teachers, but the teachers couldn't talk back to the principal. For every question I asked—why something didn't work, why there weren't any supplies—the answer was money. When I met with the staff, there was total silence, no talking, everybody just sat around and looked. I told the teachers, "You know, I'm not used to holding meetings by myself." By the end of the visit, I realized that this group of teachers just accepted things the way they were.

---

[71] Bank Street and Lippincott are two different programs used to teach elementary reading. The programs consist of graded reading books—called basals—with skills believed to to be appropriate to certain age and grade levels.

Now, I worked at a school where the teachers had everything under the sun that you would want or need. The school was an air-conditioned school; it was carpeted throughout. We had lots of parent volunteers and a group of very vocal teachers. They didn't just take what you gave them.

Finally, after I had made two or three visits, one of the teachers told me, "This place is a dumping ground for teachers. If you don't work out some other place, they send you to North Shoreview. All you need to do is look at the list of things that we requested in the last five years and we've got none of them." One of them was a parking lot that every school in the area has, one was a staff room. Now, I want you to get the picture of this: no place to park, no staff room, burned-down buildings in the yard. I thought, This is the craziest place I've ever been.

As I said I am very rebellious and very outspoken. I am not afraid to fight—I pick my battles—I fight and I fight them hard. I believe that if you just fight everything, then you won't be effective. I decided that this was a battle worth fighting for. I went down to the superintendent's office and told him that he didn't want anything done with the curriculum because there were too many other things that had to be done first.

I told the superintendent that he had to come out for a visit. I wanted him to see the boys' rest room and how it smelled. I wanted him to see the burned-out buildings in the yard. After he visited the school, I invited every board member and anybody else that I could get—something you're not supposed to do—and took them on a walk around this building. I even had a mother take Polaroid pictures of those bathrooms. Yes, I did.

In early September I attended a district principals' meeting, and we were asked by the superintendent of schools to share three objectives we had for our school. The other principals had such beautiful things that they were going to do. I spoke up and said, "I don't have three objectives. I wish that I could say the things that the other principals are saying, but I can't. I want to do one thing and do it well and it will take me all year and maybe longer to do it; that is, to physically get my school into a condition where teachers

can teach and kids can learn. And I'm not doing anything else."
There was absolute silence. The superintendent glared at me.

I told the superintendent that he knew me very well, because he
had lived with me as his vice principal for three years, and that he was
the one who had sent me to North Shoreview. I said, "The one thing
that I'm beginning to believe is that this is an across-the-tracks school.
And you know full well I'm not an across-the-tracks principal."

I got busy writing work orders for building repairs. I decided
that I was going to turn this building into a school and I dared them
to try and stop me. A parking lot was installed; every room was carpeted; a two-way intercom was installed. I threw out the old, dilapidated furniture and told the people at the warehouse that the days
of bringing run-down, second-hand junk to North Shoreview were
over. They were not going to take somebody else's junk and give it
to me. And I stood fast. When they brought any furniture or equipment, I stood at that door and inspected it. They brought furniture
for two rooms that I turned down. They finally got the message.

The administrators planned to take the insurance money from
the fire that burned down the campus buildings and divide it among
the schools so that each one could install an alarm system. I decided
that was our money. It was a hard fight, but I won. Instead of replac-
ing all of the rooms, I built two kindergarten rooms and some office
space, because that's what we needed. They weren't going to send
me to do a job, lie to me, and make it impossible for me to do the job.

After that first year I began writing curriculum grants because
I really wanted to change the school. I had conducted a survey
which revealed how little time students were actually spending
in the classroom. Most of the kids were in their classes only 17
percent of the school day. Kids were leaving to go to speech ther-
apy, to go to Title One, to go to English as a Second Language,
to go to learning disabilities.[72] This school was Grand Central

---

[72] Chapter 1 is a compensatory program designed to improve the academic
achievement of children from low socioeconomic backgrounds. Originally called
Title 1, these funds were retitled Chapter 1 in 1981. Chapter 1 funds were first
authorized under the Elementary and Secondary Education Act of 1965. Approximately 70 percent of all public elementary schools receive Chapter 1 funding.

Station. Kids were going everywhere to get fixed. When they came back to the classroom, no one knew what had been fixed because there was no coordination. All I knew was that it wasn't working. After showing the results to the teachers, I began assigning educational research. We read and discussed the research.

Some friends of mine at Johns Hopkins University had told me about a researcher, Robert Calfee, at Stanford University. I decided to call him. I didn't ask anyone's permission because I had learned that if you ask, someone is going to say you can't do it. Just do what you want to do and take the consequences, because the consequences can't be too bad. They were not going to fire me and I knew that. I was too good. I told him, "Look, I'm Ethel Tanner." I told him about the school. "The kids can't read. The teachers can't teach. I have no money. But I have a great desire for the kids to learn. And I feel that placing them in the correct environment they will learn."

All he said was, "Mm-hmm. Mm-hmm."

I didn't know it at the time, but he is a man of few words. I figured I'd never hear from him anymore. Three weeks later he called and asked me to meet him for lunch. He wanted to know what I wanted him to do, what I felt my kids needed. I told him the teachers needed to be totally retooled because they weren't teaching. They were doing their best, but all they were doing was passing out a lot of dittos, keeping kids busy.

What interested him most was my comment that most inservice sessions were useless because a speaker came, made a presentation, and was never heard from again. My idea was to have consultants placed in the school, who could retrain the teachers. I told him that I didn't have any money, but that I knew I could get some. Together we drew up a plan. It focused on language arts. He sent two interns who were stationed at the school Monday through Thursday. The interns worked with the teachers in their classrooms. Later the interns and teachers would meet; the teachers asked questions and talked about their needs. They trained teachers in various techniques: used field trips to build language skills; published student writing. The interns were the kind of people who related well with teachers, so they felt comfortable and soon got involved.

We called our program Rescheduling for Excellence. We got the first of several foundation grants. The program worked so well the university began to use North Shoreview as a demonstration school. Other schools in the district came to visit. In the meantime, teachers willingly transferred to this school. It was no longer the case that teachers didn't want to work here.

In the first and second years of the program the top administrators seemed indifferent to what we were doing. They left me alone. They didn't say we couldn't do it. We received so many requests by others to visit, we organized a summer institute and my teachers taught in it. One hundred forty-seven people attended. Our summer institute was jointly sponsored by North Shoreview School, San Mateo City School District, and Stanford. At that point, the district's attitude toward our school changed.

Many of the obstacles we faced were structural and bureaucratic. Each year schools get money—called categorical fund—from the federal Department of Education. The money comes with certain restrictions. Here's an example. Title One funds are restricted to poor children who are behind academically. Children are eligible only if they score at or below some number on a standardized test. Other children are ineligible even if their score is only two points above the cut-off score. If a school district misuses the funds it can be prosecuted. Our district used Title One funds to hire aides. In all other schools, children who were eligible for Title One left the classroom to work with the aides. Remember I said this school used to be like Grand Central Station.

Instead of hiring aides, I wanted to use the money to hire additional teachers to work in the classroom with all kids regardless of their eligibility. That meant reassigning our teacher aides to other schools. I had to go back and forth with the Department of Education, but they eventually agreed. Reassigning the aides was more difficult. First the teachers' association, then the association that represented the aides got involved. They threatened lawsuits. It was a real political battle. But I held firm. I told the superintendent and the board that I had a solution to a problem at North Shoreview, and that I wasn't running a business simply to employ people. The matter was finally settled. I used the money to hire five special education teachers. Instead of kids going out to the teachers, they come in and work with the entire class. The speech teacher, for example, works in the classroom and focuses on the children who need help. By reorganizing our resources, we've been able to reduce our pupil-teacher ratio and keep the children in the classroom.

The majority of our students are poor. Many are from immigrant families. Half of them are on reduced or free lunch; some live in motels because they don't have permanent housing. There are seventeen languages spoken in the school. But we have created a belief system that our children can learn. We have set high academic standards for kids that we expect them to meet. We have a homework policy. We expect kids to come to school on time. But we have created an extensive network of support systems to help kids meet our expectations. We have an after-school tutorial staffed by volunteer tutors that is open between three and five in the afternoon. We have a meal program staffed by volunteers. Each weekday evening families can come to the school and get a hot meal, no questions asked. In conjunction with the Samaritan House, we sponsor a clothes closet. We created a recreation program which we support with contributions.

As a black principal, I realized I wasn't reaching many of the Latino families. When I first arrived, few of them came to school, not because they didn't care but because they didn't feel comfortable. When I sent home information it was rarely returned. I found out many of the parents were illiterate in their own language. So I organized a Spanish-speaking parent group. Whenever we have meetings I'll have one section in Spanish and one in English. During the meetings we talk about what is going on in school. If there is something that requires filling out forms— summer school, for example—we take the applications to the meetings and help parents fill them out. To reach Latino parents, I developed a close association with Father Isaacs, a priest over at St. Timothy's, the church many of my Latino families attend. You could say I am mixing religion and the school.

My philosophy of education is that you have to treat the whole child. I didn't get that from any of my teacher education or administrative credential courses, and that's where schools of education need to undergo some fundamental changes. I don't believe kids are really bad. If they become bad it's because of something that society has done wrong. I also believe that part of education is teaching children to take responsibility for themselves. My view of what should go on in school also has a lot to do with my personality because I can't live in a dead place, and too often school is deadly.

Our school is successful. Our test scores were among the highest in the district, number three out of twenty schools. If I had to do it over again, I would still choose education as a career, but I probably would have wanted to become a principal sooner than I did because I feel I've been able to make the most changes in that position.

Teachers have a lot of say-so in this school. I demand quality, but they have a lot to say about how we get there. Teachers can't just do their own thing; there has to be a cohesion among the faculty. When I interview teachers what's important is their energy level and their acceptance of children. No matter what their other qualifications, I don't want them if they can't accept children and form relationships with them. I want teachers who believe in kids that the society has given up on. A lot of my teachers weren't that way when I came. But if you model acceptance, educate them, they can change. Now I have a group of teachers who are very child-oriented. Not too long ago a teacher told me, "You've taught us that we should give without sitting in judgment of the person."

The teachers have become professionals, too. Their conversations have changed. In staff-room conversations you don't hear these long griping sessions about Johnny's mother. They are talking a lot more about curriculum, what happened with a particular project they did in the morning, how it worked, what someone else did, and what to do next. They're also no longer jealous of one another. They know each others' strengths. It is a common practice for teachers to ask me to cover their classes while they go to someone else's class to observe a lesson. Now they have a lot of pride. Before they didn't have the pride, self-esteem, or self-efficacy.

What's funny about my success is that when I first applied for a teaching job in this district, they didn't want to hire me. This was a lily-white town in 1960; they didn't have any black teachers. The school board didn't want to hire me, but there was a principal who wanted to. After battling the school board, he did. The summer before school started I was away visiting my brother. When I returned, my husband told me that there had been a lot of commotion over my hiring. People had called my house and yelled, "Nigger, nigger, nigger," over the telephone. A group held a community meeting in a local church to protest my hiring. Over several days, I learned what had gone on during my absence. The more I thought about it, the more I decided that I had a right to that job and I wasn't going to let a bunch of racists keep me from it. I took the job, and the rest is history.

ETTA JOAN MARKS

Lindale is an east Texas community located ninety miles from Dallas. It is home to Etta Joan Marks.

Her entire teaching career has been spent in Lindale. Her first teaching position was in the same all-black consolidated school she had attended as a child. After nine years of teaching in a segregated school, she was one of only four teachers who was transferred and assigned to the newly desegregated schools. Her euphonious, welcoming voice belies a steeled determination. This interview was conducted in her classroom.

When I was a little girl growing up, Lindale was extremely segregated. Blacks didn't own property. We didn't make any money. The only thing that black people could do in town was work for whites. If your family worked for a prominent family, you might fare better than other black people did. But it was hard for all of us. We were black; we knew our place and we stayed in it.

I came to this school in 1965. I was teaching in an all-black school and one day toward the end of the school year I received a telephone call. The voice said, "Etta Joan Marks, get over here. I want to see you." And I said, "I can't leave now because my principal isn't here." It was the superintendent. He said, "Come. I need you now. The principal will understand."

I got in the car and left the school, which was about eight

miles out, and came over to the white school, over to the administration building. I was sandwiched between two principals, one
on one side and one on the other. The secretary and the superintendent were also there. They carried me through the wringer.
The questions they asked were ridiculous. The superintendent
said, "Etta Joan, do you know that we have to have some black
teachers?" I said, "Yes."

He said, "You are going to be very fortunate, because you
are going to be one of the black teachers that we are going to
hire." He continued, "It should make you feel very proud,
whether you do or not, that you're going to be one of the ones
who are retained. You are the best teacher that I have in the system, black or white." And he rubbed his hands, his white hands,
and said, "I didn't have to tell you that. And if you tell anybody I
said that, I'm going to tell them you lied. Do you get my meaning?" That's how it happened. That's how I ended up at this
school. His call came before school closed for the year—in the
middle of the term—because that next year we were going to
have to integrate.

I started working during that summer. We had to have summer school, a Title One Program, and they had to have a black
teacher.[75] So they asked me to work during the summer. I was
the only black teacher in the summer program; all of the others
were white. There were black and white kids. I didn't want to
work but I had to.

Before desegregation black children from Lindale and other
small towns attended a consolidated school. When the schools
desegregated, the consolidated school closed and all of the
black children returned to their own communities. All of
the black elementary school children from Lindale went with

---

[75] Chapter 1 is a compensatory program designed to improve the academic
achievement of children from low socioeconomic backgrounds. Originally
called Title 1, these funds were retitled Chapter 1 in 1981. Chapter 1 funds
were first authorized under the Elementary and Secondary Education Act of 1965.
Approximately 70 percent of all public elementary schools receive Chapter 1
funding.

us to integrate the school. So only the black children from Lindale attended Lindale Elementary. The teachers made it clear that blacks were not welcome. In the classroom the white teachers would put the black kids on one side of the room and the white kids on the other side. This is so that they wouldn't touch or mingle.

There were only two black teachers in the school, my cousin and myself. Neither one of us had a class because the townspeople didn't want us teaching their lily-white kids. But the superintendent had to have some black teachers because he didn't want to violate the law. So we went to school every day, sat in a room, and did whatever we wanted to do. We worked over half a year in the school system without teaching any students. We drew full salaries and got retirement.

After a few months the other teachers started complaining. They were upset because they had classes and we didn't. At first the principal didn't respond to their complaints. But the teachers kept complaining and, eventually, he gave us some students. We weren't regular classroom teachers. They created remedial reading classes; we became remedial reading teachers. All of the black and poor white students were assigned to the remedial reading classes. Those were the only kids we came in contact with. We only taught three classes a day because we both had to share one room that wasn't as large as a regular classroom.

The first half of the year we didn't have to do anything, and the second half of the year we taught three remedial reading classes with only nine to twelve students in them. This continued for two years. Eventually, the teachers started complaining again. They separated us, sent my cousin to another school, and I was left alone at the elementary school. The teachers treated me like dirt. I didn't eat with them. I couldn't use the teachers' bathroom; I had to use the students' bathroom.

I continued to teach remedial reading. Each year I requested a regular classroom. The principal told me he was never going to let me out of the remedial reading classes. One day I was a sitting with my head down, and the superintendent's wife, who was teaching in the school system, came by. She asked me what was wrong. I told her that I wanted to get out of teaching remedial reading classes, but that the principal told me that I would never get out and that I felt trapped. She suggested that I go over and talk to her husband, the superintendent. I told her I was worried that if I did I would be accused of not going through proper channels and that I couldn't afford to lose my job. She convinced me to go. I went over to the administration building, told the superintendent that I had been trying to get out of remedial reading and that it seemed that the reason I couldn't was because I was black. He told me that there were going to be quite a few vacancies and asked me what grade I preferred. He didn't commit himself one way or the other. He said he couldn't promise me anything, but that he would see what he could do.

The day after I went to see him, he sent the principal to talk to me. He approached me, smiled, and said, "You finally got out of teaching remedial reading. I want you to know that I bitterly fought against it." Apparently there had been a board meeting and the principal had said he wouldn't release me from remedial reading classes. The superintendent stood up and told him that not only would he release me but that he was going to tell me himself the next day.

The next year I got assigned to a third-grade classroom. Once I got assigned to a regular classroom, I began to get a lot of parental requests to have their children placed in my classes. That's when I realized that at least some parents had some confidence in my teaching ability. That was my turning point.

In spite of all the problems I encountered, I was more fortunate that many black teachers. Most of those who worked with me in the segregated school didn't have jobs. They lost their positions and had to look for new ones in other communities. Only four of the twelve black teachers were retained in the system. Besides my cousin and I, only two other teachers—the homemaking teacher and her husband, the principal—were reassigned. As for the principal, they put him in a room upstairs, said he was assistant principal and told him to answer the phone when it rang. [74]

I've taught in a segregated school and a desegregated school in the same town. If I had to compare the experiences, I would say that in the black schools teachers had to do a lot more work, but our kids were appreciated more. In the white school we get more materials, we have more to work with, but we—blacks—aren't appreciated as much. The white schools sent us their used textbooks just before they were ready to put them in the trash. Pages were torn out; they were old, worn, and so marked up that there wasn't any space to write our names. Usually when schools order textbooks, they also receive teachers' editions. We never received even the used teachers' editions. The only way we could get teachers' editions was if we ordered them and paid for them ourselves. In 1961 or 1962, when our school burned down, we didn't have textbooks of any kind. We held classes in the church. The school system didn't replace or furnish anything. If we wanted books, we purchased them. We managed with whatever we could find. We bought our own construction paper, our own scissors, our own glue, even our own Kleenex. We bought everything that we used. Until I started teaching here, I didn't know that the school system appropriated money for each teacher in

---

[74] School desegregation decimated the ranks of black teachers and black principals. One study found that 31,504 black teachers in seventeen Southern and border states were displaced between 1954 and 1970. Another study by the U. S. Department of Health, Education, and Welfare found that between 1968 and 1971 1,000 black teachers lost their positions, while 5,000 white teachers were hired. A number of other studies, some conducted by teachers' unions, others by scholars, reported similar findings. A U.S. Congressional Committee investigating the dismissal of black teachers confirmed the findings of these studies. School desegration also ravaged the ranks of black administrators. In one Southern state, the number of black elementary school principals dropped from 620 to 170 between 1963–1970. During the same period the number of black secondary school principals was reduced from 290 to 10. The effect of desegregation on black teachers and administrators was greater in small, rural communities than in larger urban communities. Not until the mid-1970s, primarily because of federal intervention, did the dismissal of black educators slow down substantially.

the white schools to spend on materials. It wasn't much—only $100. At the black school we'd spend at least $100 every year ourselves before school started, purchasing materials, and we didn't get reimbursed. There might be a record player to use, but we'd have to use our own records. We didn't have a gym. If we played ball, we had to play when the weather was good, because we could only play outside. Occasionally, the white school would let us use their gym when they weren't using it, but that was so rare.

In the desegregated school we have an abundance of materials to work with. The first time I ever got a teacher's manual handed to me with my textbooks was when I started teaching in the desegregated school. We had new classroom furniture. We were given new books, new record players, and new cassette players. It was like going into a different world. Materially things are better in the desegregated schools. But black kids have regressed instead of progressed because whites teach whites and the blacks are left out.

Another difference is the black schools were much stricter. The principal required that every teacher in the school attend every school function, activity, or outing. Unless we were sick we had to attend and be seen at every school function. In the white school, they don't care whether teachers go or not.

When I was a child, the school system required all black teachers, even those from other towns, to live in Lindale during the school year. They lived in a house near the school; it was like a dormitory. This residence rule was still in effect when I started teaching. My husband and I were going to move to Tyler because we had made plans to buy a home there. Tyler was a larger town and that's where I wanted to live. The superintendent heard I was going to live in Tyler, so he called me in. He told me that I couldn't live in Tyler and work in Lindale. We bought a house in Lindale because I didn't have a choice. I wanted to work.

At that particular time, blacks were not allowed to buy brick homes. Brick houses were considered too good for blacks to own. It was a visible sign that we no longer knew our place. We couldn't get anybody to finance our home because Lindale Bank would not finance blacks' homes. We were able to get our home because we found a company that would build a home if you had land and we had land. We didn't even have gas or city water when we built our house. We had a well. In 1960 blacks didn't have access to the city. The only way you had access to city water in 1960 was if you lived in Mr. Charlie's house or your house was behind his. We have only had gas and city water since the early seventies.

I don't know the exact percentage of black children in this community, but there aren't more than one hundred black kids in this school. Many black students don't pay attention to school, but I blame this in part on what is going on in school. Since integration they've had mostly white teachers and a lot of these teachers haven't cared about black kids. The only thing that black kids are allowed to excel in in this school system is athletics. If you're a good athlete, the teachers will try to keep your grade-point average up high enough for you to participate in the athletic program. But if you're academically inclined and black, you'll only get a C. We have a gifted and talented program here. There's only one black kid in the entire gifted and talented program in this school.

My daughter was born in 1965, the year the schools desegregated. She started school in 1969 and went up through the Lindale schools—primary, intermediate, junior, and senior. She had a difficult time here in the schools as most blacks do, even now. Having some knowledge about the school system, I knew it wasn't going to be easy for a black student, including my daughter, to excel at anything. So I enrolled her in a lot of activities in the Tyler school system. Since she wasn't a resident of Tyler, I had to pay for the activities. Every week I drove her to cooking school, sewing school, twirling school. Back then I was one of the few black mothers driving my child back and forth to these activities. She was only the second black twirler in the Lindale schools and there have been none since her. But I had to take her to Tyler for two years for twirling lessons so she would be able to participate in that at Lindale. I wanted her to do well in school and participate in school activities. Still she was never placed in any of the accelerated classes and was rarely recognized. The only thing she was ever recognized for was twirling. She received better grades in her freshman year at Tyler Junior College than she did throughout her entire school career in Lindale. She received better recommendations from college having attended only one year than she got from Lindale having gone all her life. She's not too fond of the people around here, and I don't believe she'll ever come back to live here.

A lot of her classmates didn't go to college. Quite a few dropped out. Some married in their senior year and had babies because they were never recognized. The teachers didn't encourage them, so they got discouraged. My daughter is one of the few black students who went on to college. I was determined that she wasn't going to be a casualty of the system, so I worked with her. From the time she was a little girl, I drilled the importance of school into her. She hated school but liked learning; she's always said she wanted to be a lawyer.

It has been tough going for me in this school system. Most of the parents don't give me any trouble, but over the years I have had some problems with a few white parents. Several years ago a white parent, who had moved here from the North, came in to see if I could talk. I said, "You came in to see if I could talk! What do you mean 'talk'?" My first thought was that she was a racist, suggesting that black people don't talk well. That made me angry; I was tempted to throw her out of my classroom. She told me that the previous year her daughter had a teacher whose English was incorrect, and she considered speaking correct English to be important.

I said, "Evidently, you are not from these parts." She told me she was from the North. "Well," I told her, "I assure you, I can talk. It might not be the way you talk, but I assure you I can talk." After that encounter she was pleasant to me, but she harassed the other teachers.

Another parent wanted her child removed from my classroom. Early one morning before school began, the principal came to tell me there was a parent waiting to see me in my classroom. When I got there, the woman was standing with her hand on her hip. She announced, "I want my kid out of your room." I asked her if there was a problem. "Yes," she said. "I want my daughter to have a college education, and I don't want her in your room." Trying to gain my composure, I told her that all parents want their children to go to college; and asked again whether there was a problem. She repeated her statement: that she wanted her child taken out of my classroom. I knew then it was a racial issue, and I told her that we should go to the office.

When I told the principal that the woman wanted her daughter removed from my class, he asked why. I repeated what she told me. Then he asked whether or not I wanted the child moved. I told him that I wanted her to say in my room. He called the woman into the office, and said, "Lady, that stuff you're talking about went out years ago. Mrs. Marks is not having problems with your kid; she's having problems with you. And you're having problems accepting her as she is. I will not remove your child from her room because she does not want her removed."

Last year I got the Kinsey Award, the local Teacher of the Year award. It is given at the graduation ceremony. The same principal who wanted to keep me teaching remedial reading is the one who had to give me the award. He never told me where to go to receive the award. The commencement exercise was supposed to be in our football stadium, but because of the weather they changed the location, and he never told me. He said he knew what I'd done to deserve the award and that he didn't know what he could write about me. He told me to write something about myself, and to give it to him within the hour. I proceeded to write. When I gave it to him, he tried to find errors. He said that I misspelled words, which I hadn't. Then he told me it was full of grammatical errors, but it wasn't. Each error he pointed out, I contested. Eventually I told him not to bother me.

When I got to school the next morning, I told my principal that I appreciated being nominated for the award, but that if the other principal didn't stop harassing me, I was going to tell him what he could do with the award. My principal told me that it wasn't the first time that my name had been mentioned for the award.

The night of the award, in the presence of all the white people assembled, the principal was searching for me. When I finally got on stage I sat right in front of the superintendent. They didn't give me the plaque or money that night. All I got was what I had written about myself. They didn't give me the plaque until later in the summer, and they didn't give me the check until I requested it.

In Lindale there are only three black teachers including me. The system hasn't had any black teachers in twenty years. Everyone talks about how terrible it is that there aren't more black teachers. Everyone asks why more blacks don't go into the profession. But no one ever talks about what happened to black teachers during and since desegregation. I understand why young blacks don't want to go into teaching. Given the prejudice, if they are going to survive in this white teaching world, they are going to have to be exceptionally strong.

We need more black administrators. If we had more strong, black, independent administrators things might be better. But the few black administrators that we have are afraid that they will lose their jobs and they try to appease the whites. If we are going to attract more blacks into the teaching profession, a lot of things are going to have to change.

LORRAINE LAWRENCE

The interview took place over a two-day period at Lorraine Lawrence's school and home in Orlando, Florida. She is tall, genteel, and elegant. Subdued and reserved at the beginning of the interview, she became more animated and talkative as it progressed.

She was born in Haskell, a small town in northeastern Oklahoma, and lived on a forty-acre family farm five miles outside of the town until she left for college. She is one of nine children, all of whom have gone on to successful careers. Between 1966 and 1972 she taught in Cleveland, Ohio. Named Teacher of the Year in 1988, she was serving as English department chair at the time of the interview.

As long as I can remember I wanted to be a teacher. As a child I admired my teachers because they seemed to be doing important, meaningful work, they had steady jobs, and they seemed to have enough money to live well. At the time, I didn't know that their salaries were so small. Quite a few teachers that taught at my school were from other communities, like Langston, Tulsa, and Muscogee. Because they were from out of town, they stayed with families in Haskell. Two of them boarded with my grandmother, and since we visited our grandmother's house often we got to know them personally.

I began "teaching" when I was young, about six or seven years old. My aunt Francis, a third-grade teacher, went overseas with my uncle Major, who was in the army. Before she left, she brought all of her teaching supplies—every pencil, crayon, instructor magazine, notebook, construction paper. So I had all of those things to work with, and I was so excited about it, because it meant I could teach my younger brother and sister. I had learned a few things in school by then and every day I would have my brother and sister sit in the circle, do work, and color.

All this took place on a farm a few miles outside of Haskell, Oklahoma, which is between Tulsa and Muscogee, where I grew up. Although there were a number of all-black towns in Oklahoma, Haskell wasn't one of them. The town was segregated: black people lived across the railroad track, whites lived on the other side. My father had a number of jobs. He farmed and he also was a minister who served as a pastor to two country churches. Ministers in black churches weren't paid well, so he worked in a department store and as a school custodian. My mother played the piano and directed the church choirs. Every other Sunday our family would go to one of the two churches where my father would preach. Afterward we would go to one of the parishioner's houses and they would feed us with a big spread, with baked chicken, turkey, ham, and vegetables that they grew in their gardens, and a half a dozen desserts. Before we bought a car, I can remember standing on Highway 64 that runs through Haskell to catch the Greyhound or Trailways bus. All of us would trail to the back of the bus and travel to church.

I am the oldest of nine children. I began school in a little country one-room schoolhouse, but attended Booker T. Washington, the segregated school in Haskell for grades one through twelve. My younger brothers and sisters spent part of their school years at Washington and then transferred to the desegregated school; my youngest siblings attended only desegregated schools. The school system never ordered new materials for us. When the white school got new textbooks, we got their discarded books. We had a library with a small collection of books. We didn't have a band or any of the other things that are considered essential for today's schools. The enrollment was about three hundred; there were only eighteen students in my graduating class. Mainly, we had a group of exceptionally dedicated and caring teachers who emphasized education, stressed character, and drove us to achieve.

My parents couldn't afford to send me to college, but one of the teachers at my school who was active in the Langston College Alumni Association told me about a scholarship granted to high school valedictorians. After graduation I entered Langston University. Even though I planned to major in English to become an English teacher, by the time I got to college I had second thoughts. I remembered some of my teachers in Haskell who had to leave their homes and travel two hundred miles to get a teaching position. When I entered college the school faculties weren't integrated and black teachers couldn't always find work, so I switched my major to business. One day the subject of my major came up in a discussion with my freshman composition teacher who asked me why I wasn't an English major. After I told her about my dilemma, she convinced me to switch my major to English.

One of my English teachers at Langston was Melvin B. Tolson, a black writer. He taught English literature, speech, and a number of other courses in the department. He was an enthralling teacher, not at all like the other teachers. He didn't follow a syllabus. He would say, "I'm teaching you about life." A lot of times he talked about himself, his writings, or about the content of his work, like the *Libretto for the Republic of Liberia*. He would read sections of his work and tell us what they meant. I remember vividly when he gave us a lesson in meter. He decided that the best way to do that was to have us dance. He chose me, picked a fellow and he made us dance. He'd recite, "The CUR-few TOLLS the KNELL of PART-ing DAY!" And we would step to the music. He was very dramatic. He didn't have a list of topics as a speech teacher would; he would just go around the room and spontaneously call out a topic appropriate to that student. For instance, to one student who always came late to class, he might say, "Your topic is hasten but never hurry." His style of teaching was challenging and interesting, and we learned from it. His classes were the most popular on campus 'cause he was entertaining. But there was a method to his madness. Whenever the drama department could catch up with him, he would present an evening of poetry or act in a play. Here was a great poet, who because of racism didn't have a lot of options, teaching at Langston University. Dr. Tolson influenced hundreds of black people through his teaching. Although we were fascinated by him, even we didn't appreciate him fully.

Race has always been an influential factor in my career. My first teaching position was in a high school in Cleveland, Ohio. One reason I was hired in Cleveland was because the school system was actively recruiting blacks. Ninety-nine percent of the students in the high school were black, but the staff had only a few black teachers. This was in the mid-sixties, and various black organizations were demanding that the school system hire more black teachers. When I came to Orlando in 1975 I got a position in a junior high school and later in a high school because the schools had been desegregated and the principals needed a certain percentage of black teachers. I have served as chair of the English department since 1979.

Teachers are responsible for imparting subject matter, and they really need to know a subject inside out if they're going to teach it well. But if teachers are going to be effective with students, they have to be concerned with more than simply teaching their subject matter. They have to help students see their potential, see beyond their current situation to the possibilities that are out in the world, which, because of their inexperience, students may be unable to see. In order to do that teachers have to be concerned with their students' feelings and emotions. Too many teachers have abrogated their duty.

Left to their own devices, too many black students simply choose not to participate in various activities. If I announce something in my class, the black kids say "Not me." They simply won't get involved. Teachers should make students get involved in various activities because it's good for them. When I was growing up, that's what my teachers did with all of their students. So I handpick students to participate in various activities. One year we were planning an oratorical contest for the Dr. King holiday, and we were asked to have some students enter the contest. I

didn't ask; I simply told one student that I knew he could speak
well, because I had heard him speak, and that I wanted him to
prepare a speech and enter the competition. I told him to meet
me after school. He said, "Oh, all right, yes ma'am!" Then I told
another student that one of the other teachers had told me about
her outstanding activities in her church group, how well she
spoke there, and that I was going to enter her into the oratorical
contest. She agreed.

It reminds me of a conversation my younger brother, James,
who has a Ph.D. in medical research and who is also a physician,
and I had about six months ago. He came to visit me on a weekend while he was here attending a national conference, and it
just so happened that I had an oratorical contest to judge at that
time, so he went with me. Afterward we were talking about our
experiences in school and he remembered how he had hated a
particular teacher we called Professor Johnson because he
would make him sign up and speak at every oratorical contest.
Professor Johnson would make him write a speech, help him
practice, and take him to all of the little country towns in Oklahoma to participate in oratorical contests. Even though my
brother didn't want to go, our parents backed the teacher and
made him go. He told me how grateful he was that this teacher
had forced him to participate in these contests because now he is
able to present findings from his research without any problems.

I had similar experiences when I attended school. If a teacher
was going to have a program, she would assign a student the
introduction. One day a teacher told me that I was going to play
the piano. I dared not tell her that I couldn't because I hadn't
been practicing or that I didn't want to do it, because she would
just say, "I know you can do it," or something like that. Those
black teachers just made us do things that they thought were
good for us. I find myself doing more and more of that especially
with my black students.

I can see a difference between today's students and the ones I
had when I first began working. My first teaching position was as
a student intern in the Muscogee Training School in Oklahoma,
where I took over for a teacher who was ill. The students were

so happy that I was there, they were eager to learn and receptive to what I had to teach. Today's students are more jaded, and I have to work much harder to win them over. But I manage to win them over by treating them fairly, not harshly. Over the years, I learned that I can handle almost every situation and most students by being rather gentle with them. Yet I still accomplish what I need to.

One of the main criticisms of today's integrated schools is that the black youngsters do not get pushed enough. In my high school, the few black youngsters in the honors classes, who are highly motivated and capable, who are active in school, tend to be more affluent. They go out for cheerleading, drama, and debate; they run for student council and get elected. The majority of black students—those in the regular group—are generally left out. They aren't cheerleaders, they aren't in the choir, which goes on tour every spring. They just don't get pushed to the front.

What I notice about these students is that they are capable of doing many things and many actually do quite a few things in the community and in church. Many of them play instruments and they are in singing groups, but this tends to be outside of school. Too often their teachers don't know anything about black kids' lives outside school, so the teachers conclude that these kids don't have anything going for themselves. If the students had a little encouragement, they could not only participate but excel in extracurricular activities.

In order to teach well, I think you have to think about students as if they belonged to you. If teachers showed the same concern, interacted with their students and treated them as if they were their own children, schools would have more success with greater numbers of students. Instead, teachers sit in the workroom and complain about the kids, how they aren't very smart or how aggravating they are. In class they discourage students, they are punitive, and they teach in such a way that the student hates the subject. In my years as a teacher and as department chair, for example, I have seen teachers ridicule students who receive a bad mark, and seat the class according to the grades they receive on a test. It's far too common for teachers not to expend any energy working with students who are labeled "slow learners." These teachers will complain about whatever the students can't do. But teachers ought to be able to work with a student no matter what the level.

The very best teachers can get all students to achieve. These teachers don't waste time complaining about what students can't do. Instead, they create the classroom conditions that enable students to achieve. More often than not, the students singled out for the most punitive treatment, the students considered the most aggravating, the students labeled slow learners are black. This is a serious problem that has yet to be dealt with satisfactorily in desegregated schools.

When I get together with people from Haskell and Langston, we often talk about the many positive experiences we had as young people growing up in these communities. People who don't share this past wonder how anything positive could have gone on in segregated communities. Some people charge that we are romanticizing segregation. Other people claim that we are calling for a return to a racially segregated society. I am not romanticizing segregation, and I certainly don't want to go back to those days. But there are lessons that can be learned from my experiences and the experiences of thousands of other black people like me who lived under segregation. Our teachers could see our potential even when we couldn't, and they were able to draw out our potential. They helped us imagine possibilities of life beyond what we knew. These teachers knew that most of the students sitting in their classrooms were from small towns and that they had not had much experience, but that they had good minds, and with adequate preparation they could learn and achieve, and so they worked with everybody on that basis.

Even though the black community no longer lives under legal segregation, thousands of black children could still benefit from studying under the kind of teachers that taught me. Too many of today's teachers seem incapable of visualizing positive futures for their black students. So they can't help black students conceive of and prepare for futures that go beyond their present circumstances. All of the current debates about how to prepare teachers have more to do with the academic credentials teachers should possess than with the personal qualities that are required to be effective educators. Most efforts in education are aimed at developing better ways to test teachers' knowledge of subject matter. There is no question that teachers have to know the subject they plan to teach. But the kind of changes needed in education will not come only from having teachers better trained in their subject matter. We've got to devise ways to determine which teachers can develop the empathy and understanding necessary to reach all students, but especially black students. Until we do that we're going to continue to have large numbers of black students fall through the cracks.

EDOUARD PLUMMER

Edouard Plummer was born in West Virginia and attended West Virginia State University. He has been teaching in Harlem at Wardleigh Junior High School since the early 1960s. In 1964 he initiated a rigorous program to prepare Wardleigh students to take the Secondary School Scholastic Test and be placed in prep schools across the United States.

Describing him, one of his students wrote: "He has the fervor of a revivalist minister, alternately threatening damnation to those who fall by the wayside and promising salvation to those who keep the faith and follow his gospel." He has the same passion for literature, art, and the theater, whose artifacts are in evidence throughout his tiny midtown Manhattan apartment.

I attended Dunbar High School in Washington, D.C. Dunbar was on a par with any school in the country, black or white.[75] The

---

[75] Originally known as the M Street High School, Dunbar High School (named for Paul Laurence Dunbar) was the first high school for blacks in the nation. At the turn of the century, it was the only black public high school in the country that prepared black students to enter industry or college. It had an excellent reputation and produced many of the country's leading black figures. Its goal was to prepare black students for college and produce a cadre of blacks who would provide leadership to the race. Many of its faculty had advanced degrees from Northern and Eastern colleges. Mary Hundley, *The Dunbar Story, 1870–1855* (New York: Vantage Press, 1965); Thomas Sowell, "Black Excellence: A History of Dunbar High" *Washington Post* April 28, C3; Hines, Brown and Terborg-Penn, 1993, pp. 276–278.

education I received in segregated schools was a good one, primarily because of the interest of the teachers, teachers who are willing to go above and beyond the job. That experience is what has made me do the same thing in my teaching career. When I say the teachers went above and beyond, I mean they were interested in you as a human being, in your future. They went out of their way with you as a person, to give you advice, to help you, to talk about your family problems or personal problems. They were not afraid to help you. These teachers wanted you to move ahead, they believed in you, and you were able to believe in them.

There's a lot of controversy today about whether or not teachers or schools should try and teach values. If teachers are just there for the dollar, then they are not going to bother. But if they are there as human beings and see the children as human beings, then teachers can't avoid teaching values. Teachers work with young minds, and if they are molding these young minds for the future, then they can't avoid teaching values. In my case, I was taught values along with academics, so I do the same thing. When my children come in in the morning I stand at the door and I notice and talk to every child who comes in the classroom. If they have been absent I want to know why they were absent. There's usually a reason for these things and I try to find out if there is something I can do to help. The children know they can *always* speak to me in private about anything they want to. They know I am always available.

I know all about the evils of discrimination. I majored in history, political science, and minored in German because I wanted to go into the diplomatic corps, but that was unheard of for blacks at the time. I read in the newspaper where they were holding meetings for people who were interested in the diplomatic corps, so I decided I would go and present myself. When I arrived at the hotel, they were shocked because I was black and trying to go in the front door. I asked for the room where the interviews were being held and when I walked in you could see the shock on their faces. I was the only dark person there. I stayed and went through all the sessions and the preliminaries, gave my name, address, phone number, and other information they requested. Of course,

I got a polite letter a few weeks later essentially saying, "Thank you very much, but at this time we are unable to consider you for employment"—one of those nice letters, "thanks but no thanks." That experience hit me square in the face. But all I could do was accept it as one of those things—the way things were at the time. After college I went into the army and served from 1952 to 1954. After the army I lived in Europe for a few years.

I became certified in an unconventional way. I came to New York in 1957. At that time I still hadn't decided to become a teacher. But I was broke and needed a job. A friend of mine—actually, a classmate from West Virginia—was teaching in New York. I wanted a job, and I went to visit him at Wardleigh Junior High. Until then, I had never thought about teaching, but my friend introduced me to the principal, and after we talked he told me he thought I would make a good teacher. I began teaching at Wardleigh and it's the only school I've ever taught at. Of course, I was required to take courses in education in order to get my certification.

Although I had taken psychology classes in college, I had never taken education courses. In general, I found that the education course were useless. They taught you some techniques. But what you need in the classroom is the ability to think on your feet, some knowledge about the students you are teaching, and some imagination. The only course I found at all helpful was math. The course not only taught me how to teach it but it helped me get a better understanding of it. I like mathematics, and I make children like it for the first time. A lot of parents tell me, "My child likes math for the first time!" And I felt very pleased about that.

Now they are encouraging liberal arts majors to go into teaching because some people believe they make some of the best teachers, better than those who specialize in education. In my case, I had the experience of living, traveling abroad, military service, and I have been able to bring all of the experience into the classroom.

I am a teacher who, first of all, is committed: one who is concerned, one who is interested in developing young minds, and one who sees the importance of this development. Not only for the child and his future, but for our society. I am willing to put forth as much time and effort as I can to help any child to succeed. I want the child to want to learn and to want an education. I want them to learn how to appreciate an education, not only for the sake of getting a good job but for learning for learning's sake, for the beauty of learning and knowing they can explore any avenue they want, once they have learned. This is what I want to impart to young people. If you are a learned man you are a dangerous man, but if you are an ignorant man you are no threat at all. Not only will you be a slave to white people, but a slave to any type of vices that come along. Mental slavery exists right here today, among our people. But I let children know that there is no such thing as instant education. Education is hard work, and sacrifice, but it's worth it. Hopefully as children get older, and mature, they will learn how to fight things on a different level. They have to learn to fight with their minds not with their fists all the time, because brains triumphs over brawn.

Thirty years ago I started my own scholarship program. I saw what was happening to many of our young black children, especially our young black males, and I wanted to do something different. I felt I had to do something to save these young black boys because they are so bright yet so vulnerable. Something within me was awakened. I saw the need for this kind of program. At that point, I felt that teaching just wasn't enough.

Initially I thought about going into guidance. But since I wasn't certified, the school system told me I was ineligible. So I took some, courses in guidance. This was around 1963. A friend of mine taught at Cheshire Academy in Connecticut, outside of New Haven. That year I went up to visit him, and he told me that they had scholarships for minority children. Then in the summer of 1964 there was an article in *Time* magazine that discussed new programs for minority children. It described A Better Chance, a program started in Boston. When I read about the program I knew that this was exactly what I wanted. It just fell right in my hands, like that. So, over lunch one day I talked to all the black teachers on the staff at Wardleigh. I showed them the material and talked to them about my plans. They said they would support the program and then I went to the principal. I told him about the program and gave him the material to read.

The next day when I asked him what he thought about the program, he said, "You think you can get some of *these* children in *those* schools?" I could tell from his reaction that he had no confidence in his staff and worst of all he had no confidence in the students because they're black and Hispanic. I was angry. I wondered who this white principal thought he was. I stared at him and said, "I know I'll get some children into *those* schools." He had challenged me and the other teachers in the school. He asked me who was going to pay for the tests that the children had to take. I gave him the names of all of the black teachers. That was our demonstration of Black Power. Black Power was intelligence.

We started preparing our children immediately. We went through the list and picked out the children, seventh- and eighth-graders, high-achieving children. We called them in for a meeting, told them about the program, discussed the opportunities of going to private schools. The children looked at us like we were from another planet. We told them to tell their parents everything we had told them and to give them the material. Eighteen parents agreed to have their children participate. This was in September and the test was scheduled for December. We started working after school on test-taking skills. We helped the families fill out applications. On the day of the test we were all there early. The children took the test, completed the application, and sixteen of the children were accepted to prep school. This stunned the principal. The story made the front page of the *Amsterdam News*, the local paper here. The *New York Times* did a big spread on us. Our first year began in the fall of 1964 and the story was printed in the spring of 1965.

Years later a few of the children who had graduated from college told me, "Mr. Plummer, we thought you were crazy. We only took that test because you asked us to. We didn't believe we were going to prep achool. We didn't know what prep school was at the time." They had no confidence in themselves at that time, but I did. From the beginning I was confident about what I was doing.

The students went, they finished, and most of them are doing well. They call themselves the Pioneers.

Eventually the schools started coming to us because they read about us in The *New York Times* article. We have had our detractors, those who speculated we would not last. People think I'm doing the public schools a disservice by taking the children out of public school. They accuse us of only taking the cream of the crop.

We work with the children every day after school. We run a six-week summer school program. They study English, mathematics, and test-taking skills. The graduates of the program come talk to them. Over the years the alumni have become more and more involved. The veteran parents talk to new parents to let them know what it's going to be like. Once the children get into prep school, they know they can call me collect from their school anytime they want. Parents can call me anytime they want; I'm available twenty-four hours. Over holidays we have a meeting. We meet again in March and in June.

As far as I am concerned, this program has been where I have made my mark. Of course, I haven't done it all by myself. A lot of other people have supported my efforts. They have provided financial and moral support. When people have told me I shouldn't be involved in sending kids out of their community, I think, Why shouldn't blacks get the best education possible?

We've had some bad moments. Even though I would like to have a hundred percent success rate, we haven't. Nineteen eighty-five was a bad year. At the end of March a young man who finished Hotchkiss School (a prep school in Connecticut), had graduated from the University of North Carolina, and was a second-year Harvard Medical School student, was killed in a car crash. It nearly killed me when they called me. In June of the same year Edmond Perry, one of our students who was attending Exeter Academy, was killed by a policeman. I have another student who was in the program who is now in Sing-Sing for murder. He left the Hotchkiss School to come back to the city, became involved in selling drugs and executed someone. He ended up in prison. But I like to dwell on the positive achievements of the program; most have been positive. The first thing I ask any of my young people—once they've gone through preparatory school—is whether it was worth it. The majority of them say that it was because they see what the experience has done for their lives.

I am especially interested in what happens to young black males. In too many black homes, if there were boys and girls in a family, and it came to who would get an education, who would go to college, it was always the girl; never the boy. Parents hoped the boys would make it on their own. How can black boys make it on their own, compete with those white boys who have gone to college, and everything, to get anything? Black men were frozen out of the trade unions. We can't make it on our own. Too many families have the idea that they have to save our black girls, but who are our black girls going to marry? We have to overcome the false impression that black boys can't be scholars. That's ridiculous! I don't know where that idea came from. But it's wrong and it has to be corrected. Black boys internalize the idea that they can't become academically successful at an early age. We have to educate our young black men if we are going to make progress. Today if the black male reaches twenty-one, that's great. If he gets to twenty-five, that's a miracle.

When blacks emigrated to the great urban areas, the family structure came under attack. New York is the great equalizer, but it is also the great destroyer. There are more opportunities for advancement as well as for destruction. Which of these two roads are our children going to take? I don't care what anyone says, black people need an education. Even more now than ever in this world of technology. We have too many functional illiterates out there.

The biggest reward I get from teaching is seeing the achievements of the young people, seeing them succeed. It's a pleasure to know that I helped to mold them. Nothing is a greater reward than that. It makes me feel so proud. When I read about their successes, when I see them, or hear them speak, I just beam all over. Their achievements make all the blood, sweat, and tears worthwhile.

It sickens me to see some young black children with these hostile, negative attitudes walking in the halls and classes, being so cocksure of themselves. Little do they know that they are nothing but walking death at that early age. It's so demoralizing, especially knowing I cannot do anything about it. It leaves me frustrated and depressed. These children think they are supposed to do as they please, and they believe that no one is supposed to try to reprimand them or tell them to get on the right track. These children are participating in their own destruction. They are destroying themselves, they are destroying others, and they don't seem to care. In fact, they think it's funny, they laugh. They cannot read or write. That is the irony of it. They can't see that they have been programmed for failure. And I know where they are going to wind up. They can't see it, but I can. Experience is still on my side. Not every black child is going to preparatory school, and not every child is going to the university. But they must find something to do. The black community needs tradespeople; we need businesspeople.

At the same time the school has changed, the teachers and administrators have changed. They come in with this "I don't care" attitude about the children: "I have mine, you get yours." A few teachers are committed. There have always been people who are not committed, but it seems like more of them are coming in now as teachers. These teachers try to get down to the children's level, to be like them. We don't need that. We need role models. We need good, positive-image black role models. Too many teachers let the children do as they please. They let them sit up there, laugh, talk, and play. Then our children cannot compete with their children. That's the irony of it. James Baldwin used to say that teaching black children is a revolutionary act.

If different options had been available to me in the fifties, I wouldn't have gone into teaching. During the last twenty years, I've watched doors open that were closed to us. That's why I've encouraged young people in my program to go through those doors that are open to them.

If you want to teach in urban schools, you have to assert your position each and every day. You have to let the children know that you are the one in control of the classroom; that there are certain things they have to do and you expect them to do. Consistency is very important. You may have to repeat the same phrase over every day, but do it until it sinks in. But you can't make demands of students and not be prepared as a teacher. Teachers have to be prepared to teach every day from the time they walk into the classroom until the day ends. Let them know that education is important. Let them know that they are preparing for their future. Let them know what is ahead for them. Let them know that you are there to teach, and they are there to learn, and not that you are not going to let them stop you from teaching. Give them work every day, but make the work important, even the smallest assignment, make it important. Have something significant for them to do the moment they get there in the morning until they leave at the end of the day. Work them hard, give the work back, and give praise when they do well. When they don't do well, let them know. Expect something of them. Don't go in there without expectations, because they have been programmed for failure from day one.

Teach them the classroom routines, rules, and the reasons for them. The reason only one person talks at a time is so everyone can listen to the question, everyone can benefit from the answer of the question. That's how they learn and how they can learn from each other. Let them discuss things, but in an orderly manner. Be at school every day because, if not, the children get the idea that you don't care. Let them know how important it is for them to be in school and to carry themselves with dignity and pride. Be fair. But let them know that there is a difference between the student and teacher.

If I had the power to reconstruct schools, I would change them from top to bottom. First, everyone would be accountable, starting with the principal on down. You start at the top. If you have a good top, then you can go on down. If the teachers cannot pull their weight, they should be out. Those who aren't teaching should be given the support to learn how to teach effectively, but if they didn't improve within a year or two, then they would be out.

Where children are seriously behind academically, they should be in smaller classes where they can learn, where they can be given more individual attention. Parents should be made accountable for their children. As black people we must have an education. That doesn't mean that as black people we won't still be put down, frowned upon, made fun of. When I talk with children, I try to be honest about that. But education does give you some options. What options do black people have without it?

Without an education, what are black people going to be? If we can't read, and we can't write, what are we going to do? Without some type of training, without discipline, without self-control, without motivation, without drive, inspiration, or integrity, morals, values, what are you? These aren't old-fashioned values. These are the values that made us strong people. It made us able to endure being brought over on slave ships, survive the voyage, survive slavery. It made us survive the Ku Klux Klan. There's more coming and our children will have to be better than we were to survive it. I have survived, I'm a survivor. Black people have survived. But will our children survive? I don't think what I am doing is old-fashioned at all; I am saving little black souls, teaching them how to survive.

MILLICENT BYARD GRAY

Students call her "Mean, mean Mrs. Gray." She teaches biology and is chair of the science department at Vachon High School, an all-black school with a mixed faculty, in St. Louis, Missouri. A photograph from the 1966 high school yearbook shows a bright-eyed, attractive woman with flip hairstyle and a mischievous smile. Except for a slightly fuller face and white hair styled in a pageboy, Millicent Byard Gray looks the same. She wears a white lab coat over conservative business clothes.

The thirteenth of sixteen children, her grandmother Jane was a slave. In 1974 she was chosen as Missouri Biology Teacher of the Year. We talked over dinner and later in her classroom.

I've been at Vachon High School so long, many of the kids and parents see me as part of the building. As a result, I have a reputation at the school, one that has been established by whatever the older students or parents have said about me. Having been at Vachon since 1966, I am now teaching the children of some of my former students. There's one little fellow that's a grandchild; his grandparent was our Parent-Teacher Association president. I taught their daughter and now I am teaching the daughter's son. Many of the parents tell their children, "I just hope you get Mrs. Gray." They come up to school and tell me that they want their child placed in my class. I assure the parents that their children will be all right; I'll watch them at school. I'll be their mother at school and they can be the Mama at home.

Vachon is an inner-city school with a variety of kids. Some of the kids have problems and some of them don't. But the majority of students want discipline, guidance, and adults who will steer them and give them some direction. I know this is what they want because many will come back later and tell you that you were one of the few adults that made them do what they were supposed to do. They are thankful you made them do the correct thing or that you didn't take no for an answer. They may stick their tongues out when you do but we adults and teachers can't let that bother us.

I am exactly like the teachers who taught me when I was a child. In Kansas City in my time, the schools were segregated and all of the teachers were black. There was only one high school for blacks—Lincoln High School; all of the Negroes, as they called us at that time, went to Lincoln. The black community was close-knit. All of the teachers knew the parents and the students. In those days when you got a job teaching, you taught forever. That's what I've done. Just like my teachers knew my parents for a long time, I know the parents of my students.

Although my reputation precedes me, before they come into my class the students don't know what to expect. Of those who are assigned to my classes some want to have me as a teacher, others don't. I always tease those students who haven't been in my class. I say, "How did you go through Vachon for four years and didn't get me as a teacher? Once you get out there in the world, you're gonna meet people like me, but you will not have had any practice and so you won't know what it's like."

The students at Vachon call me "Mean, Mean Mrs. Gray," but if I had to describe myself I would say I am a no-nonsense person. I am serious by nature. When I first meet my students, I tell them that it's all right if they don't like me, that I am not responsible for them liking me, but that I am responsible for teaching them. I am their teacher and don't necessarily want to be their friend. They know that whether they like me or not I will still make them do their work. Once students get to know me they find out that I am not so bad. What really upsets some of them is discovering that they actually do like me. A lot of them will come to my class during lunchtime or after class just to talk.

Students learn that there's a fun side to me as well as the mean side they have heard about. Once, when the teachers had a talent show, we had a little chorus line and I was on it. In order to generate some excitement about the upcoming show, we decided to put on a preview. I thought about what I was going to do at the preview to get the kids interested in attending. Remember, the students all think that I am a mean teacher who doesn't believe in having any fun. I put on a pair of shorts and I had a long shirt that I pulled way down so that all you saw was the shirt and a pair of blue tights. When they pulled up the curtain, we all had our backs turned. I turned around and boogied, danced just like they do. Did I have a party! That night we had the show. I performed the way I was supposed to, but the students were surprised when they saw me perform in the preview.

Over the years I've made it a habit to get involved with students beyond the classroom walls. Sometimes I do academic things with them; other times the activities are more social, and sometimes I combine the social and the academic. When I teach an anatomy class, I take them to the medical school with me on Saturdays. I conduct the anatomy class at the medical school, and they have a chance to work with the cadavers. I take students to the zoo. Sometimes I accompany them to games, and afterward we might stop at the library. In the past we used to do more things together on Saturdays, but recently the students seem less interested. I try to build excitement about the trip by talking it up in class. A few weeks ago there was a Saturday seminar for science fair projects. I told the students they could learn how to do science fair projects, but even if they weren't interested they would still have a good time. I told them that afterward we would go for pizza and sodas and that if there was still time we would walk over to the zoo. Only four out of eighty-five wanted to go. On Monday those that went came up and thanked me. These trips are designed for the students and me to get to know each other better.

My classes are relaxed, but I don't let students believe that classes won't be demanding or that they won't be held to high academic and behavioral standards. When students first come into my class, I let them choose where they're going to sit, and I make my seating chart from that. I let them know that they can have a say in the seat that they chose as long as they participate in the classroom. If not, then I reassign them to a new seat. Most of the students don't want me to do that. I introduce myself and lay out the ground rules—that we aren't in school to play games and that we should all strive to be fair with each other. I discuss my expectations: they have to be to class on time, bring the materials they need, and come with an attitude that is conducive to learning.

Teachers can't hope to help students develop academically unless we are dedicated to nurturing the personal characteristics that will help them succeed. Working with young people to develop academic and personal skills takes an inordinate amount of patience. While I have a lot of patience, sometimes mine is shorter than I would like. But I do know what I want them to achieve, how I want them to do it, and we work from that. I try to get students to realize that they need to internalize whatever they are learning, and not worry about the grade they will get.

When you ask most high school teachers what they teach, they will respond with a subject: science, mathematics, or English. High school teachers don't talk much about teaching students. But in order to teach effectively, teachers have to teach more than their subject. My focus on teaching students rather than my subject comes from my experiences as an elementary school teacher. I teach them about life. This includes appropriate and respectful ways to interact with me and with the other students. They have to speak to me when they come into class. Some of them are in the habit of just saying "Hi" or just nodding their head. But I insist that they talk to me and to each other. I also work with them to overcome habits that won't serve them well in the future. I have had several students who were extremely shy—one boy I remember in particular. Together we worked on combating his shyness. We would talk on the telephone, and he would practice giving me answers. We would meet after class. After a year he was able to speak up; he could express his ideas confidently, he felt positive about himself and his abilities. That's what I want all my students to be able to do, to look at me and others in the eyes, not in a defiant way but with some self-assurance that they know and believe in what they are saying. The young man wrote me a fantastic letter in his senior year. It said that I was the first person that he met that just didn't accept his being shy, but helped him to overcome his shyness.

Compared to the students I taught in the sixties, today's students are passive. School doesn't seem to mean anything to them. In the late sixties and early seventies, students were angry, restless, and defiant, but this behavior had more political overtones. Even if they didn't, it was easier to redirect toward positive goals. At that time, black was beautiful. Being black meant students had to know and read about their background. High school students were being influenced by the political activity in the community—newspapers, demonstrations and rallies—and this activity would spill over into the classroom in productive ways. You would hear students talking about what Malcolm X had said or what Muhammad Speaks had written. Students would argue about political and social issues. You almost never hear today's students talking about these issues. They don't seem concerned about such things. I remember once when the students at this school went on strike and they boycotted classes. One day the students created quite a disturbance by setting some wastebaskets on fire. But the point of their boycotting classes and creating the disturbance was to get more courses that were relevant to blacks. The point of the unrest was essentially positive. The heightened political consciousness affected what went on inside the school. Both the community and the students seem to have lost that political orientation.

The teachers and the administrators also seemed more interested in what happened to students. Teachers were more likely to insist that students go to class and follow up when they didn't. Some of those administrators then were a little stronger than the ones we have today. They weren't as likely to cave in to teachers' demands, especially when they knew that those demands weren't in the best interests of the students.

Today I find myself constantly trying to find ways to reach students to show them how what they are learning has meaning to their own lives. One of my ways is through career awareness, to expose them to careers related to biology, not just being a doctor or a nurse, which is all that the students know. By the time they leave my classes they know about a variety of science-related occupations—science editors, various kinds of medical technicians, pharmacists, agronomists, and physical therapists.

Students are required to do a lot of group work in my classes. That's to build responsibility and group cohesiveness. During the lab work they assume various roles. One role is that of technical adviser. Another student assumes the role of secretary. Another, who is responsible for gathering all of the materials, is the coordinator. Each student has to assume the responsibility of the role. Together they work on the various experiments. While they are working, I circulate, asking them to explain what they are doing. I ask them questions but don't tell them the answer, because I want them to grapple with the problem. I want them to be able to justify what they are doing and be able to draw conclusions from the set of data they are working on. Sometimes I sit at their table, observe them, and don't say anything. My goals for students are pretty straightforward. I want the students to develop some stick-to-itiveness in terms of achievement, and most of all to develop their minds.

In order to expose the students to the library, I used to require that they get a library card from the public library, go to their neighborhood library, and check out a book on a topic we were studying. But the last principal said I was asking too much of students, so I stopped requiring that. Still, I think they need to become familiar with the library, and while I no longer require it I encourage students to go to the library. The library has a project that they are working on with the St. Louis public schools on Saturdays: how to write term papers and things like that. But it's harder to get the students to go down to the library to get a library card, and impossible to get the principal to back me up.

There is one big difference between what I have to do and what the teachers taught me in Kansas City. They didn't have to expend as much effort getting to know the parents. Because the black community was much more cohesive and close-knit, teachers were much more likely to see parents in their day-to-day activities. I really have to work hard at getting parents involved. Early in the year I make calls and introduce myself. During the first few weeks of school I call each parent. I make a card for each child's family. Sometimes the parents think that their child has done something wrong, but I assure them that I am just calling to introduce myself.

I also send out a letter. In the letter I introduce myself and tell parents that I believe close contact between parents and teachers is important to their child. I tell them the kind of things that we will be doing in class, what their child should do, what they can do to help, and tell them how to contact me. I outline my expectations. Most of the parents are very cooperative. The school has parent conference days when the parents come to pick up their child's report card. If the parents don't remember receiving my letter, I give them another one.

Once the initial calls to parents are made, I set aside some time every evening to make calls to students' homes. If students are absent from class, I call home. I tell the parents that I didn't see their child in class, and I am calling to give them or the child the assignment. Often I call and talk with kids. I might discuss a homework assignment or explain a concept that the student didn't seem to grasp in class. If students seemed upset or were misbehaving in class, I call them to try to get to the bottom of the problem and solve it before they return to class the next day. I note the date and the time of every call and whether or not I made the contact. This keeps me aware of what is happening with my students. It helps me break down barriers, establish positive and working relationships with parents. Parents are very cooperative. They want their kids to learn, do well in school, and they are proud when their children achieve.

When I first started teaching at Vachon, we had much better parent participation than we do now. The teachers were more willing to reach out to the parents even if it meant going to where the parents were. When the Pruitt Igo Housing Project was in existence, the teachers used to go there and hold the PTA meetings in the community room. We served refreshments. All the parents had to do was come down to the room; we had a whole roomful of parents. Now parents rarely come to the meetings. The parents have their reasons for not coming, but the newer teachers aren't interested in reaching out to parents. Too many of the teachers at my school are only interested in themselves, their personal problems and issues. And they seldom think about how their issues affect the school community.

Not too long ago a group of powerful, influential teachers convinced the principal to hold parent-teacher meetings in the auditorium. These teachers claimed that they were afraid that parents might become angry and violent. They insisted that the conferences be held in the auditorium to insure teachers' safety. Even though there has not been one instance of parents becoming violent with teachers, they were implying that black parents are antagonistic and belligerent. Unfortunately, because the principal is afraid of these vocal teachers, he agreed to their request. These same teachers were able to convince the principal to hold two different faculty meetings, one after school and one in the morning to accommodate those teachers who can't stay after school. Teachers ought to be able to clear their calendars to attend one meeting a month. But many of these teachers don't really want to be here. All they want to do is get tenure and move on to a better school. I call Vachon School "the training school" because we provide training for teachers who want to move on to better schools and to principals who want to move into central office administration.

My father was the son of a man from an influential, white Virginia family. When my grandmother, whose name was Jane, got pregnant, the family didn't want to be reminded of his indiscretion, so she was sent to Arkansas. Everyone knows how those masters used slave women. That's how my father ended up in Arkansas. His father did pay for him to attend college. But even with his college education my father never got a decent job. He did a little bit of everything: he sold automobile tires; he was an auto mechanic; he taught my brothers auto mechanic skills. During the Depression, he had a business washing and Simonizing cars, and he taught my brothers how to Simonize cars. They did the work, he was the inspector. For a while he worked at the *Kansas City Star* on their paper route, and all of the children would pack papers. He did a little bit of everything to make his "three nickels," as we called it, to take care of the family.

We lived close to the library and every Saturday my mother took us to the library. My mother and all the children went together as a family. In those days if you could write your name you could check out books. We would choose our books, stay and read them in the library until the library closed at noon, and then walk home. My father always took two newspapers; one was his and one was for the rest of the family to read, and we knew better than to mess up his newspaper. He wasn't that talkative, but he would talk to us about what we had read in the newspaper. His influence on our learning was more indirect than my mother's.

Our older siblings paved the way for the rest of us. My oldest brother was intellectually gifted. By the time he was eleven or twelve, he had read Plato, Spinoza, and Machiavelli. He was so smart that he participated in a study on gifted children. Since my brother had that kind of reputation, when the rest of us came along, many of the teachers expected that we would be as smart as he was. The rest of us were average.

I attended Lincoln High School like all of my brothers and sisters. Lincoln was a renowned high school and had some great teachers. Many had graduated from Harvard and Yale. The teachers at Lincoln High School were black but for the most part they were light-skinned.

There was a lot of color consciousness in my community and in my school. I'm the brown-skinned child, one of the darkest children in my family. As I told you before, I am serious, and even as a child I was serious. The neighbors used to comment: "That little dark one, she's too serious; we need to watch her. She doesn't laugh when the rest of them laugh." In those days people equated being dark-skinned with being evil. I always resented that.

Although I have had lots of opportunity to advance, I never wanted to be an administrator. I want to be a classroom teacher, because I believe that I have much more independence as a teacher. You control your classroom. You determine what your objectives will be, what part of the curriculum you're going to cover, how you are going to cover it, and if you are a competent teacher you know whether or not students are learning.

I have a lot of ideas about how we might improve student

achievement. We need smaller classes. We need "master" teachers to teach students who have the most difficulty learning. We assign the most inexperienced teachers to work with the most challenging students. When I first came to Vachon, they had the tracking. In most schools, beginning teachers get the lowest tracks, so I was assigned track three. I had come from teaching gifted and talented students, but it never mattered to me what level I taught. After teaching the lowest tracks for about five years, getting good evaluations and achieving good results with students, I was promoted to working with higher-level students. But I always volunteered to teach the most challenging students, because I thought I had a lot to offer them. Most teachers don't want to be bothered with these students. At our last department meeting, I made the statement that all the best teachers and all of the department heads ought to teach a class with the most difficult and challenging students. The best teachers should be assigned to the students that have the greatest difficulty with school because presumably these are the best teachers. Department heads should also teach these students because we can't help teachers if we haven't dealt with the challenge ourselves.

One of the most important things I have learned about working with students is that you can't react to everything they say or do. Students will sometimes call teachers names. What does that mean? When I was teaching six-year-olds, a child called a teacher a "black SOB." The teacher was white. She was so upset that she came over to me to tell me. The kid was six years old. I told her that the child didn't even know what a black SOB was. He had probably heard some people say that and the child repeated what he heard. I told the teacher that the child didn't know what he was saying. In this school some of the students will call the white teachers racist. But they generally do that when they are trying to get out of doing something that they should. I try not to react to everything the students say, and whenever I can I turn what they say into an opportunity for them to learn something. One day when a student called me old and gray-headed—a habit they have—I pointed out a student in class who also had gray hair. We talked about why we both had gray hair. Was it pigmentation? Did it have something to do with heredity? I was able to turn this incident into a lesson.

I don't spend much time in the teachers' lounge because most of the teachers spend their time complaining about the students. In the past, when I heard teachers talking so negatively about the students, I used to try to get them to change their attitude. Now I don't go in there because I don't want to hear all that negative talk. With all the things I have to do, I don't have the time. And I realized after many years of trying that I wasn't changing any teachers' minds.

Although teachers ought to be able to determine what to do in their classrooms, they have to be accountable for teaching the subject, and until we are willing to be accountable for teaching all of our students, regardless of backgrounds, we aren't going to get the kind of respect we want. Not too long ago I had an experience that shows part of the problem. In our department we are supposed to administer a departmental biology final examination. When I asked the other teachers in the department to submit questions for the final examination, I got questions like "name the parts of the microscope." Here it was the thirty-eighth week of school, and teachers are submitting final examination questions asking students to name the parts of the microscope? That isn't the kind of question that should be a part of a biology examination. That kind of low-level expectation that too many teachers have of black students made it impossible to seriously consider most of the questions. When I submitted more challenging questions, the teachers responded by saying that the questions were too difficult and that the kids couldn't answer them.

Overall, I have felt that the advantages of desegregation have been outweighed by the disadvantages. One definite advantage of desegregation is that it gives the individual the opportunity to go to any school. But the way desegregation has been implemented makes me question whether it has really benefited rank-and-file black students and black teachers. St. Louis has a desegregation program that buses students from the city to the county. Black teachers and students face hostility, discrimination, and racism out in the county schools. Most of the people in the county schools don't respect our abilities or they expect us to be experts on everything black.

A friend of mine is one of the black teachers they recruited to teach. In the district where she teaches, they had twelve kids that came in from the city. The teacher was a biochemistry major. Prior to coming to St. Louis she had taught college-level science in Louisiana. Out in the county they had her teaching five science courses to seventh- and and eighth-graders. They not only had her teaching the youngest kids, but they placed all of the students who came from the city in one of her five classes. Black teachers out in the suburbs always got to prove themselves.

One of my students transferred from Vachon to one of the county schools under the desegregation program. He told me that during class when the teachers asked questions they ignored him; they never called on him. One day the teacher was asking about parts of the cell. He had his hand up, but she didn't call on him. Finally, after calling on the all the rest of the students and getting the incorrect answer, he spoke up and said he knew the answer. So he named the parts of the cell and their functions. The student said that the teacher was amazed that he knew the answers and asked him where he had learned it. He told her that he had learned it at Vachon High School in his biology class. The teacher was surprised that a student from the city schools could be so well prepared. It is impossible for black teachers and students to function under such intense scrutiny.

The most rewarding thing about teaching is seeing students outside of school. Seeing current students downtown, and having them recognize and want to talk to me always pleases me. Occasionally students who have graduated come back to visit to tell how and what they are doing. That makes the job worthwhile. One young man came back to see me recently. He said, "You won't remember me, I graduated 1966."

"Oh, you're older than I am," I joked. When I asked him what he was doing, he told me he was working for McDonald's— McDonnell Douglas. He told me that the teachers at the school had done something right.

It's always a treat to hear how I have been a part of a student's success. I do believe that if teachers are positive about what they are doing, eventually most students will come to understand that you are interested in their growth and development.

PAMELA OTIS OGONU

Married to a Ghanaian architect, Pamela Otis Ogonu is the mother of two daughters. Her high school students call her Mrs. O. A colossal ornamented Christmas tree stands in the corner of the living room. She tells me she is planning a big Christmas celebration for her daughter, who will be coming from her first year at college.

In 1981 she was the first black person to be chosen California Teacher of the Year. She was graduated from Knoxville College in 1964 at age nineteen. She has a master's and doctorate, both in education.

The Samuel F. B. Morse High School is a large school—almost 2,300 students in grades nine through twelve—located in southeast San Diego, which is the black section. There are two predominately black schools in the city; one is Morse, the other is Lincoln High School, which has 700 students. It was once a primarily white school, but about twenty-eight years ago, blacks started moving to the Skyline area, where the school is located. When I began teaching there twenty-six years ago, the school had an almost completely white administration, but there were more black students than I had ever seen anywhere else while I was substitute teaching.

The area has been in transition for a number of years. Blacks were the first to move into the area. They were followed by Filipinos, Laotians, and Vietnamese. As the school population changed throughout the seventies the school experienced a lot of racial unrest: the kind of problems that a lot of schools undergo as they become more and more racially diverse. The school hasn't had problems for a decade. I enjoy teaching at the school because I like the diversity. My primary concern, however, is with the black students because there are so few black teachers in the school.

From a very early age I knew I wanted to be a teacher. When I was about seven or eight, there was this man from South Carolina who couldn't read, just as my grandfather couldn't read, and I taught him to read. I was just a young child and the idea of helping an adult, who was so eager learn to read, was a powerful influence on my wanting to teach. When I graduated from college at age nineteen, I felt unprepared to teach because I felt that in order to be a teacher and to have something worthwhile to give to pupils, you had to have had some experiences yourself. How was I prepared to teach anyone? It just didn't seem right to me.

Most of my professors assumed I would go straight to graduate school. But instead, after graduation I joined the Peace Corps, because I thought I was too young to teach and I wasn't interested in going to graduate school. This was during the Kennedy years when the slogan was, "Ask not what your country can do for you. . . ." I bought into that idea. So after graduating in June, I went home for two weeks and then went straight to the University of New Mexico for an entire summer of Peace Corps training. We did Outward Bound and survival-type exercises; we studied the language and learned about the culture, the history, and geography of the country. There were about a hundred of us in the program, but after the training there were only forty of us left. In my whole group there were only two blacks, me and Marilyn Downey, a girl from Texas. Most of the white people were from elite schools like Yale, Berkeley, and Harvard who were taking time off before going to law school, medical school, or into politics. These people were telling me about their fathers who were lawyers, doctors, and accountants. A lot of them had traveled all over Europe, lived here and there. I had never been anywhere except Knoxville and to little church conventions in Florida. But none of this meant anything to me. At the time I was too naive to know that these schools were supposed to be important.

After training from June through September, we went straight to Brazil. I was sent to Sape, a small town in northeast Brazil, in the state of Pará. I was stationed with a Jewish guy who had grown up in San Francisco. For two years we worked together in a public health program. I worked as a midwife. Delivering babies was my primary job, but I organized a mothers' club where I taught health. We were really health and community development workers, so we vaccinated babies and conducted health and nutrition workshops.

Being surrounded by Afro-Brazilians gave me a heightened sense of my blackness and it changed my whole perspective about where I fit into the world. The experience expanded my world view, introduced me to pan-Africanism, taught me to be flexible and to respect other cultures.

As soon as I got back from Brazil, the Peace Corps asked me to go to San Francisco, and for a year I traveled all over the West Coast, working as a recruiter. The following summer I went to work in Washington. Then at the end of that year they asked me to go to Boston and become the deputy director of the Peace Corps office, working under the director, Peter Walsh, a guy who had graduated from Harvard and later went to work for the Justice Department. I worked for the Peace Corps for two years, until 1968. In May of 1968, my fiancé, who had just completed training as an architect, and I married and then moved to California.

For three years, I stayed at home, and after getting bored I began substitute teaching. At that time we lived in a predominantly white area, and I was working in all-white schools. One day I was sent to Samuel F. B. Morse High School in San Diego, which is where I teach now. I asked myself where they had been hiding this school. Although I don't know what the percentage of black students was at the time, there were more black students than I had seen in any other school. As I looked around, I noticed that they didn't even have any black teachers at the school. The second day I was there, the principal called me in and asked if I would stay because they really needed me. This is in 1971. At first

I told the principal that I wasn't looking for a full-time job, but later I decided to take the position. I'm in a school that has a faculty of 102 and has a black student population of about 48 percent and the last I counted there are only ten to fifteen black teachers. We do have a black woman principal. But in our district black teachers make up only about 10 percent of the 5,000 teachers, and this is in a district that is almost 50 percent black.

What is worse is that too many black teachers aren't doing anything worthwhile. For example, not too long ago I talked to a group of black educators. After the talk one woman, who has taught for a long time and is close to retirement, raised her hand. She said that she sat in faculty meetings for ten years listening to white teachers say that they could not teach the same curriculum to the black students who were bused in because the black students couldn't do this or that, and that for a long time she just sat there, listened, and didn't say anything. The teacher confessed that not until nine years of hearing conversations such as this did she finally disagree with what the other teachers were saying. A lot of black teachers for whatever reason are just not challenging the other teachers or speaking up on behalf of black children. These teachers aren't providing the leadership we need. In my school nobody would ever carry on about black children like that if I am in the room because they know better. As black teachers we have got to make our presence felt. We owe it to black children to speak up on their behalf and to keep the other teachers honest.

In 1981 I was selected as Teacher of the Year for the State of California, the first black teacher to be selected.

For three years I was on a state commission on the teaching profession. This was a real high-powered commission in the state of California. It was primarily composed of businessmen—gray-haired white men who run America—two teachers including me, and two black people including me and Maynard, who was the editor of the *Oakland Tribune*.

While I was on the commission, we dealt with everything related to the teaching profession in California. People from all over the country came in to give talks and I read a lot of educational research. I consider that to have been a peak experience in my life, one that changed my outlook.

It was during these years that I began to give serious thought to the changes I would like to see in education. Teachers should be given more freedom and flexibility to teach the way they want. We teachers need to be given sabbaticals, and we need a career ladder. Teachers need a career ladder so that they don't have to become administrators in order to move up the ladder. Education is the only profession that has stayed the same way for a long time, and because it's the only profession that everybody has been touched by, when it comes to teaching, everybody is an expert.

Teachers should definitely be paid more money, especially if the public expects their expertise. But if teachers make any demands, especially monetary demands, they will have to be held accountable. While I don't disagree with holding teachers accountable, I fear that accountability will be measured by an increasing reliance on standardized tests, making education even more like business than it already is. Schools will be indistinguishable from the production line. Teaching will be like making Toyotas, and teachers will be paid by the number of students who do well on standardized tests. Let's say teachers were paid $70,000 a year. The expectation would be that one hundred out of your one hundred students would have to score on a particular test. Some proposals have already been made to pay teachers of poor black children more than teachers of wealthy white children. Teachers who agreed to teach in certain areas would be paid more: "combat pay" is what I call it. At first this sounds like a good proposal, but a lot of people in the black community including me reject the idea; the implication is that black children are more difficult to teach than other children.

It is impossible for me to separate my background from who I am as a teacher. Much of who I am is having people who always believed in me and guided me, whether at home, at school, in the church, or in the larger community, teachers from elementary school through college who really committed themselves to my development: Mrs. Davis, my English teacher who wrote "lines for living" on the blackboard every day and discussed what they meant for how we should live our lives. At the end of the school year Miss Pascal, my sixth-grade teacher, called each person in the class up to her desk, sat us down, and had a frank discussion with us about what she thought were our strong and weak points. We were all getting ready to go into junior high school. She called me up and told me how I could best capitalize on my strengths, and overcome my weaknesses. This was an all-black school, with all black teachers and students. Whenever I'm dealing with my own high school kids I remember these teachers and find myself doing similar things. This is where black teachers are critical when it comes to black kids. There are some things I might be able to tell them that a white teacher might have difficulty conveying, because the students assume that the white teachers are getting after them for the wrong reasons.

Other important influences on my life were the older black people at the church, people who would give me a dollar and say, "Pam, take this up to— where are you?—Tennessee? Take this up there with you, baby, and if you need another dollar, be sure and call me." Many of these people had not had the opportunity to fulfill their own dreams, and they saw me as a symbol, even as a child, somebody who could carry out their aspirations and dreams. I live with the dreams, aspirations, and commitments of my home community every single day of my life.

The least rewarding thing about teaching is the general lack of respect for teachers. I'm not talking about students, but the low status given to the profession by society. People don't have any respect for teachers. The general disregard for teachers has affected teachers. Whenever you go to a public gathering, where there are people from all professions, you can always tell the teachers because they're always the ones with their heads down when people ask what they do. In this society, where everything is based on materialism and you work in a low-paying profession, there's no way people are going to look up to you and say what you're doing is worthwhile. After all, this is America. Worth is equated with money.

I got into a lot of trouble over this subject back in Miami from an interview I did. After I became Teacher of the Year, a reporter from the *Miami Times*, a black weekly newspaper, called me. She wanted to talk about my perceptions about teaching and spent quite a bit of time talking on the phone. When I mentioned that I understood why blacks weren't becoming teachers—because teaching didn't have that much to offer young blacks—she wrote the entire article around that one point. The title of the article was "Ogonu Says Blacks Should Not Enter the Teaching Profession." The black community in Miami was in an uproar. My mother's phone was ringing off the hook. There was nothing I could say to defend myself. Unless the profession changes, unless people accord teachers more respect, what does teaching have to offer a young bright black boy or girl?

People go into teaching because of altruism, but teachers can't live on altruism alone; their altruism needs to be supplemented with a decent salary. When people point out that numerous teachers worked under those conditions in the fifties and sixties, I remind them that back then no one was making any money and other opportunities were closed to blacks. Conditions of teaching need to change with the times.

For several years our school district has been moving toward a core curriculum for all students. Most of the impetus for the core curriculum came from a black woman school committee member who felt that black students were not getting into appropriate classes. What was going on in our school district was typical of many school districts: All the white students were in advanced classes and all the black students were in basic classes. She argued that black students weren't getting an education with much substance, whereas the white kids, and the one or two black children who were in advanced placement classes, were getting an enriched curriculum. This woman fought long and hard to establish a core curriculum. As a result of her work six schools began piloting the core curriculum and Morse was one.

All students take the same courses. The result is that the number of classes offered in our high school was cut down. For example, we used to offer a class that I taught—for seniors who were having difficulty in the regular literature class. Now we only offer English literature and world literature for seniors. Regardless of their reading proficiency, every student takes one of those classes because all students are supposed to be exposed to the same curriculum.

A core curriculum presents dilemmas. Originally, in our school, faculty only wanted to offer English literature, but they knew I would never stand for that. English literature is boring and it isn't inclusive, so they are also offering world literature. Another problem is what teachers do with students who aren't as well prepared as other students in the same class. Personally, the change has not affected me. I've had to be a little more creative in grouping students to keep all students involved. But many teachers don't know or don't want to know how to structure their classes to accommodate students at different levels, and many students have been struggling in these core curriculum classes. To address the problems, I've been involved in a program tutoring students before and after school.

For most of my career I have been pleased with my students. There were one or two years when I was dissatisfied with my students. During those two years I often thought about leaving teaching, because I felt I was fighting against too many things and losing the battle. What bothered me was the way my students seemed attuned to the world of fast money, that they weren't able to see beyond the gold chains or the Mercedes with the gold rims. It distresses me when black students tell me that they don't need an education because they can sell crack and make money. Look at the people in the community whom today's black children idolize. Too many of them are enamored of drug dealers or athletes. I've just seen so many kids, smart kids who are just taken in by these false prophets. Several years ago there was a funeral for a drug dealer in Oakland and people were standing and waving as if at a parade.

When I was a child, our parents, teachers, and other community members made it clear to us who our heroes ought to be and why. When I was a little girl I used to go to visit my great-grandmother, who was one of the greatest influences on my life. On the walls in her house were pictures she had cut out of *Ebony*. All these pictures used to fascinate me. There were pictures of

Jackie Robinson and Roy Campanella. Even though some of the people were athletes, they represented more than that: They were symbols of individuals who had broken the barriers imposed on the black community by the larger society.

When adults talked about Robinson, their emphasis was not only on his athletic ability. My great-grandmother would say, "There's Jackie Robinson: He's the first black man to play baseball." All I heard was that he was the first black man. At the time I didn't see Jackie Robinson only as a Brooklyn Dodger; I saw him as someone who had broken the color barrier. That was how our communities interpreted the meaning of these individuals' achievements. They were able to play with our minds in a positive way. But today when a white person tells black students about Michael Jordan, they say, "You see Michael Jordan. He can run. Can you see how he can run?" Unfortunately, today's kids think that the reason these sports figures are important is because they play sports. This is why it is important that our community maintain control over the information being conveyed to our children.

LERONE SWIFT

Tall, lean, and lanky, Lerone Swift does not appear much older than the high school students he teaches. Affable and easygoing, he is proficient in verbal repartee. Before we talked, his wife and young daughter joined us for dinner at a local restaurant. He grew up in a working-class community in the northeast section of Washington, D.C. After failing tenth grade, he transferred to a high school in an affluent section of the city, outside his neighborhood. There, for the first time, he encountered the children of professional blacks, children who were being prepared for college and profes-sional careers. After high school he took a year off from school before enrolling in the District of Columbia Teachers College. In 1988 he was one of three outstanding teachers featured in a Washington Post *series of articles on life in McKinley High, a school with problems that are typical of many schools located in urban areas.*

I am part disciplinarian, part cheerleader. My demeanor is relaxed and my personality is very outgoing. I smile a lot; the kids used to call me "Smiley." I tend to be upbeat and to let the kids get to know me as a human being. When I see them in the hall I always take the time to talk with them. I ask them about their families, what's going on in their lives; I'll notice and comment on some things about them, like the clothes they are wearing, who their girlfriends or their boyfriends are. I try to find out what makes these kids tick. I can't deal with them as if they are numbers. No matter what students say, I listen carefully and respect what they are saying. Even if their comments are negative, I try to turn them into the basis of a positive and productive conversation. When the kids get to know me as not just their teacher, they are less likely to act up in class and more likely to cooperate with me. Developing these personal relationships prevents a lot of problems and makes it easier for me to get something accomplished in the classroom.

It is important for a classroom environment to be warm, safe, and accepting. Getting to know the students and letting them get to know me is part of helping students feel that they can trust me. Students also need to feel they belong to part of the larger group of students. If I see a student off in the back of the classroom I might say, "Why are you sitting in the back there as if nobody loves you?" That's the cheerleader aspect of my personality, but it is all part of establishing discipline.

A lot of students accept others' definitions of what they can and cannot do. I want my students to realize that no matter what they want to accomplish they can do it, to realize that the only thing that separates them from getting ahead is their own motivation. I want them to believe that they can be mathematicians, if that's what they want. Too many of them believe the lie that only Asians are good at math. I want them to believe that they can be anything they want to be, if they are prepared to put in the time. If they are willing to spend the time in the math books, then they can become mathematicians. Black kids—black people—can't allow anybody to define their potential for them. They have to believe that hard work pays off, that they can achieve if they work hard, and that no matter what their status in life they can make it better. Most of my kids don't have professional parents, and they are unaware of the opportunities that are out there.

My approach is to instill discipline first because once I have established that as a foundation I can work on the academic areas. I demand that kids respect themselves, me, and one another. Students have to respect one another. That is non-negotiable. They can't talk about one another. When somebody speaks in class they must make eye contact with the person. When somebody says something, they are never allowed to laugh or to put them down.

I treat students with respect. No matter who the student is, I believe we can always reach a common ground, a common point where we can get along and work together. My students respect me. A lot of teachers don't understand that you can't do anything without respect and discipline. You've got to demand respect in a respectful way.

Learning is a two-way process, but most of the students who come into my classroom think they can learn without being actively involved in the process. One of my greatest strengths as a teacher is my ability to motivate students to understand this. Each and every day I come to school prepared to teach them and I want them to come to school prepared to learn. I ask the students to trust me, to keep their minds open, and become active participants in their own learning. If they do those things, I can guarantee them that they will be successful in my classroom. Even though I explain the reasons at first, many of them don't fully understand what I am asking. Throughout the year we assess the progress they are making. But it isn't until much later that they come to see that there's some method to this madness.

Another strength that I bring to the classroom is the insight I have gained over my life. Many of the things that the students are going through now, I've experienced on a firsthand basis. Like many of my students, I wasn't a good student in high school. I have run my own business and can tell them what it's like to be in business for yourself. I can tell them about other aspects of life as well. What it's like out there just hanging around the streets. I can speak their lingo, so to speak. I'm much more conservative in my approach than I have been in the past. The world has become less forgiving than in the past, and, though it is unfortunate, most of the kids I teach are not going to get a second chance.

I did my student teaching at McKinley Technical School. It was one of the few schools in the District that had technical programs, where kids came and majored in science and math. At first, teaching was difficult because I thought teaching was like preaching. Telling students what was right and what was wrong. A teacher *told* students what history was about. When I look back on it, I realize I wasn't doing much teaching. I was giving the students a lot of information. But I don't know if I gave them much of an opportunity to learn anything. At the time, I didn't have any way of assessing their learning. My teacher preparation had taught me to give the information, not necessarily to get the students to learn it. There's a big difference.

It took me a while to realize that I wasn't actually teaching. My first teaching assignment was at Rebough Jr. High School. Rebough was considered the best junior high school in Washington D.C., and I felt fortunate to be hired there. I stayed there six years and that was where I began learning what it meant to actually teach. One day the principal, who was black, observed me. He was one of the finest principals in the school system. He had a feel for everything in his school. He knew how to provide structure, how to provide discipline, how to handle his subordinates, and he didn't do it in a heavy-handed way, but there was no doubt about what he wanted.

The day he observed me was a Monday. Sunday night I had gone somewhere and partied. I didn't have a lesson and went in there totally unprepared. During the fifty minutes, he was observing, I was scrambling. I even asked the kids to hand in something I had already collected. A few days after he observed me I went to pick up my paycheck, and when I asked the secretary for my paycheck, she said, "Mr. Swift, Dr. Graves has your paycheck." I asked her why.

When I went into his office, he said, "You ought to sign this paycheck over to the school system, because what you did in there wasn't teaching. All you did was talk. Talking is the worst kind of teaching. Kids don't remember anything they've heard or been taught. So, just sign your name. I'll take the check and return it to the District, because you didn't do anything." What he said really shocked me. He burst my bubble. From then on I became more self-critical.

The next year I began to look at myself as a teacher, doing a self-inventory and evaluating my own performance. He gave me the chance to look at myself and to see what I was actually doing. He helped me learn that there is more to teaching than just talking and preaching. It is not just giving information. It is being able to determine if students have learned. What good is it to give a student information? So he can write it down in the notebook? So you can say that the kid took good notes on a particular day? How do you evaluate their learning? How are they growing? It wasn't until I got to McKinley High that I understood many of the demands that this principal had placed on me and the importance of what he was trying to convey.

It's been in the last six years that I have really fine-tuned the art of teaching. Now when I teach, I want students to be able to evaluate ideas, analyze and synthesize material, write a position paper, debate an issue, come up with hypotheses, argue and defend their ideas. Knowledge is worthwhile only if students can do something with it. I want them to develop some skills that they can use and apply outside of school. Do students know what the conservative agenda is? Do they know what the liberal agenda is? Do they understand what America is all about? Do they understand capitalism? In order to understand these issues, they have to able to analyze things. Years ago, learning was one way: It came only from me. Now in my classes, learning flows in many directions and across many subjects. I want to see students using some of what they have learned in English in my history class. I'm a different teacher today than I was at the beginning of my career.

I grew up in an area of far northeast Washington, where very few of the people were college educated. Most of them were blue-collar workers, but even in our community of workers they all insisted that young people respect one another, show some discipline, and try hard to get ahead. The philosophy in my elementary school reflected the community's values. Parents and teachers didn't tolerate any nonsense. If things weren't right at school, the parents were the first ones there to get them corrected. They didn't wait for any bureaucracy to respond. They took care of it right then and there. Our parents considered education a lifeline to a better future. If you had gone into those schools, you would have seen black kids achieving academically, working hard. There was a seriousness of purpose. The principal, the teachers, and the kids were black. This was a black school with high standards. The teachers were firm and they made you do what they thought was right. We internalized this firmness as caring about us.

The junior high school I attended served children from a larger area. The kids in my junior high school came from a broader ranger of socioeconomic backgrounds. Many of them came out of public housing projects, but others came from neighborhoods where most families owned their own homes. The school was run by a firm, strong principal who didn't tolerate any foolishness, so there was no way that students were going to act up in her school. It didn't matter where a student came from, once we entered that school, everyone was on their best behavior.

Throughout my elementary and junior high school I accepted the importance of education, which was the dominant and prevailing view in my community. It was in high school that I had problems. I attended two high schools, the first year at Spingarn. Spingarn was in the northeast and it was the feeder school for my junior high school. My older brother, who was a year ahead of me, had gone to Spingarn and had made quite name for himself academically. He was much more academically oriented than I was. When I got to Spingarn, I didn't want to be known as Lee Swift's brother. I wanted to be completely different from my brother, so I intentionally rebelled. Spingarn also drew its students from an area much larger than both my elementary and junior high schools, so I was meeting kids from different neighborhoods. The peer pressure got to me; I decided that in order to be accepted I'd be "one of the boys." I purposely came to school late and didn't do any schoolwork. There were times in algebra class where we would be in the back of the room shooting craps. Tenth grade was such a disaster that I had to repeat it.

When I returned the following year I still didn't do much of anything. But I knew that I needed to get away from the negative peer influence at Spingarn. In order to do that I ended up transferring to Roosevelt. I wasn't sure where the school was located, or even how to get there. It was in the Gold Coast area of the city where the black professionals, the "muckety-muck" of Washington, lived. Roosevelt gave me some insight into life because the school served students who came from families with professional backgrounds, the children of doctors, lawyers, dentists, and real estate agents. These kids had been exposed to a much different lifestyle than I had. Starting all over again, at a different school, trying to find myself, get settled, and make a name for myself meant that the tenth-grade year was a lost year. Eleventh grade was a bit better, but I still wasn't exactly serious about school. But the standards of education were much higher at this school. The teachers were better, they took more of a personal interest in students, and the parents made sure that their children got everything they needed to become successful.

The parents and teachers in this neighborhood believed that the only way their children could become successful in life was through education. These parents had lived through segregation and had managed to overcome the limitations of segregation through education. And they preached education to their children, and their children internalized that message.

Floretta Dukes McKenzie, who later became the superintendent of the District's school system, was among this group. The teachers were the "Sojourner Truths" and the "Mary McLeod Bethunes" of our generation. They fought the battle of segregation and had felt the pain. Many of the things they imparted to us came directly from their experience of what it was like trying to get an education. We were the generation that benefited because they passed their experiences directly on to us. It was the early sixties. When they talked to us they used to make it clear that we had to pursue education because the battle was against white folks and overcoming segregation. They told us that we had to be better, because it was only through education that we would be able to sidestep discrimination.

At Roosevelt, there was definitely elitism, because the parents only wanted their children to come in contact with a certain kind of black. I began to compare the goals of my neighborhood high school—graduating from high school, working hard, getting a car—with those of Roosevelt, and I could see a huge difference.

Neither of my parents had finished high school, and they didn't gear me to go to college. They just insisted I not break any laws, not engage in any criminal activities, and finish high school. Going to Roosevelt where the emphasis was on finishing high school and going on to college was a definite eye-opener and an important turning point in my life. The main reason I decided to go to college when I graduated in 1966 was because of something the father of the girl I was dating said. He owned a real estate company in the Gold Coast. He took me aside and told me that anyone who was dating his daughter had better enroll in "some man's college."

When I graduated from high school, I stayed out a year and went to night school to improve my grades. The next year I enrolled in D.C. Teachers College, a predominantly black school with a rich history and a solid teacher-training program. The school had a fine reputation for producing excellent teachers and had graduated the bulk of black teachers in Washington, D.C. Like a lot of students, I went to Teachers because it was affordable. I didn't do much my first year or second year. At the time I was not career-oriented. I was not looking down the road to the future or thinking of the day in which I would get out. For the first couple of years, I was just treading water. I got in and out of academic trouble a couple of times. Quite a few of the professors were from the "old school." They believed that teaching was a noble profession. Fortunately, the teachers believed that people find themselves at different stages in life. So when I finally got my life together, the professors at Teachers were there to help me. They were willing to challenge me, bring out the best in me, and help me realize that I had a lot of talent if I was willing to work hard to develop it. All I had to do was to work hard.

During my last two years I became serious and, once that happened, there were no courses too difficult to pass. I made the Dean's List. For me, Teachers was a sanctuary because the teachers helped me find myself as a student, as a person, as a man.

Most urban public schools need radical surgery. In order to turn urban schools around we have to begin by holding everyone accountable. If students in a particular school are not achieving academically, then those schools should be closed down. Take the teachers who have demonstrated the commitment and the ability to teach and send them to other schools. If certain teachers aren't doing their jobs, let them find other careers. School boards are a large part of the problem. To my way of thinking, the situation would be better if we did not have politically elected school boards. Too many school board members are only interested in using their position as a stepping stone toward politics. The nature of politicians is that they are primarily interested in getting reelected. Most politicans want control, status, and power, and nothing else. Several years ago the school system decided to set minimum standards. There is never any discussion about maximum standards. As the parent of a daughter who attends the public schools in this city I want my child to achieve maximum standards. When you set minimum standards, too many students and teachers only aim for that and nothing more. Another problem is that middle-class parents have abandoned the school system that benefited them, that provided them with the opportunity to advance and become successful in society.

Kids don't respect teachers today. Some of that is deserved. Teachers aren't aware of the conflicting signals they send young people. We can't verbalize one thing and send an entirely different signal through our actions.

Teachers should have a variety of things to offer kids, have something of substance, of value and benefit for every student in the class. Even though we may want students to move at the same pace, they don't. In today's schools there are some kids that can't read, but teachers still have to have something to offer them that will meet their needs. Even if a kid is weak in something, teachers shouldn't water the material down to the point that it is meaningless. Students, especially urban black students, can assess if a teacher is genuine or not and if they have something to teach. These students can read people, tell if they are genuine, in fifteen minutes. Teachers can't fake it.

If teachers aren't prepared to set high standards, hold kids accountable, motivate kids to rise to meet their standards, then they shouldn't be teaching black students. A lot of teachers can't teach black students because they don't know or understand black people, how to motivate black kids, or anything about how to build self-esteem in black children. By building self-esteem, I don't mean making individual students feel good about themselves but making them aware of their history and of who they are. If a teacher's attitude about black people is that they are shiftless, that they don't want to get ahead, that teacher shouldn't be in the classroom teaching. If a teacher has an understanding of black people in an historical perspective, that we are survivors, that we are hard workers, that we want to achieve and be successful, then they are prepared to teach black kids. But if the only thing teachers know is what the media has portrayed us to be, then they have no business teaching our kids.

JOELLE VANDERALL

Joelle Vanderall began teaching in the Boston public schools in 1952. She remembers when the majority of black teachers and students were segregated in a few schools located in one section of the city. After the schools were desegregated in 1974, she was transferred to a formerly all-white school in the city. There, she endured the bigotry of white teacher colleagues who refused to interact with her as well as the prejudice of the parents whose children she taught. She also witnessed the antagonistic behavior of the teachers toward the first black principal assigned to the school.

During the late sixties and early seventies both of her children participated in a voluntary urban-suburban desegregation program undertaken in Boston in 1966, but she has chosen to send her grandson, for whom she has primary child-rearing responsibilities, to the public schools in Boston because she feels that black students need to interact with other black students. This interview was conducted in her home.

A teacher has to be concerned with much more than academics. As a black teacher teaching black children, I am just as interested in the kind of people that my students become as with what they are learning. Many of my students come from neighborhoods that are devastated, communities in which drugs are rampant, where people haven't got the money they need to survive and they see no way out. Before, black people had more stability, jobs, and some hope. But now welfare has created a permanent class of expendable people without hope who can always be used as scapegoats by the politicians and the larger society. When the city does begin to take better care of a particular housing project, you can be sure that the plan is to move black people out to areas where they will only be barely able to survive. Relocating black people to less desirable areas in the city has been going on for years and it continues to go on in Boston.

So today, more and more black people are forced to operate outside of the law. Women are hustling to make money because they can't manage when collard greens cost a dollar a pound. People are selling drugs because that is the only way many poor black people can manage. I know parents who never let their children out of their sight, who keep their children with them all the time, because the housing projects are such dangerous places. Many of the children I teach have to deal with problems that would overwhelm most adults. Some of them have serious health problems or they come to school hungry. I have had children tell me that they were absent because a cousin got shot or their father went to jail. If some of my children are angry, if they have a chip on their shoulders, it is because they are dealing with serious situations.

Teachers always talk about the need to build children's self-esteem. But I have found that the best way to build self-esteem in children is to insure their success. That's why I emphasize reading and writing in my classroom. Because I have found that once the kids start doing well, they feel better about themselves, and that is the basis of self-esteem. And once children begin to achieve academically their parents seem more willing to invest in their children's success. From years of experience I have learned that when kids are not doing well a lot of parents are not willing to put in the time to help their children. Some of the parents feel they can't afford to invest their time in their children only to be disappointed later. Others aren't sure exactly how to help their children achieve success in an area where they haven't succeeded. I encourage parents to visit my classroom, sit down, and hear some of the children read. If their child is not reading well, I'll invite that parent to listen to a child who is reading well. That way they will have a model by which to judge their own child's progress.

The media has had a tremendous effect on life in the black community. From the time these children are born, they are being made into consumers. These kids want the best jeans, the best brands of sneaker, the latest hairstyles, the latest of everything. These kids refuse to wear sneakers unless they are name-brand sneakers, and this is in the first grade. These kids evaluate the clothes and hairstyles of their classmates. I have had children in my class criticize or refuse to play with other children because they don't have the latest hairstyles. They will say, "Miss Vanderall, look at her hair; she doesn't have a jheri curl." With all the emphasis that society and media have placed on the acquisition of the material, it shouldn't surprise us when a fifteen-year-old kills someone to get a stylish jacket. As a society, we are only reaping the disaster that we have sown. In my classroom I find myself addressing character and values much more than I ever did before. I spend time talking to the kids to get them to realize that sneakers, jeans, and hairstyles do not the person make. I am constantly reiterating that they can do the academic work.

When kids become less hostile toward each other and learn to get along with their classmates, when they have learned that there is a routine to life, when they have learned that they have a responsibility to other people, when they have learned to accept praise, when they are more receptive to learning, then I feel we are on the way to accomplishing something. When they are ready to leave my class, I hope that they have learned to see beyond grade one, to see that the things they are learning in the classroom are prized and valued wherever they go. If they can read what is written on the blackboard, they can read a sign in a store. If they can apply what they are learning in my classroom to the walls beyond the classroom, if they are ready to accept the challenge of choosing more difficult tasks instead of the easiest ones, then I feel they have the initial building blocks for success in school.

One of the ways I encourage reading is by reading the children stories during the day. I read stories in the morning as they are settling in for the day; I read again when they come back from lunch; and I usually read poetry before they go home. Reading aloud to children is very important because it is the natural way to build vocabulary. Literature also helps the children become familiar with the cadence of reading. Later, when the children read out loud, I ask them to read the way I have read to them. No matter the method of teaching reading, children have to be read to aloud. This is an especially effective approach for black children who come from communities where they are surrounded by the cadence, rhythm, and melody of language. I am not comfortable with basal readers. The stories are inane, irrelevant, and some of them are downright stupid. They aren't multiethnic.

My relationships with parents are fairly productive. I believe in maintaining contact with parents, so I call parents and keep calling them until I make contact. If I don't get them at home, I call at work. If I don't get them in the morning, I call at night. I call until I reach somebody. If I can't get reach them by telephone, I go and visit them at home. Too many teachers patronize parents, refuse to get involved with them, and hide behind the union to avoid developing productive relationships with parents. A lot of parents have told me—and I have witnessed it myself—about many instances where a parent will come to a classroom unannounced and a teacher will simply ignore them. If a parent is standing in my doorway, whether they have an appointment or not, I invite them in to sit down and watch what's going on in the classroom, because it is critical to convey the message to the parents that they are a part of the child's success.

Parents are more distrustful than they were when I first started teaching, but given the problems and the difficulties facing parents their response is understandable. After all, everybody in the society is less trusting than they once were. That means I have to work harder to convince parents to trust me. And that's why I place so much stress on getting my children to be successful with academics. Parents and children will cooperate when they realize that you are doing the right thing by them, that you are not demeaning their integrity, that you are not insulting their intelligence. Those are really basic to developing working relationships. At the same time, I am honest with parents and children because I let them know what I think.

The biggest challenges I have had have been dealing with white, not black, parents. When white children were first bused into formerly all-black schools, I had parents whose children didn't want to associate with their black classmates. And I have had white parents challenge what I was teaching in my classroom. Several years ago, I taught the children the Hughes's poem "I Am the Darker Brother" to recite in a school assembly. One white parent hit the ceiling when she found out that her child had recited that poem in public. But I told her that black people have been learning and reciting white poems for all these years and that it was time for white students to learn the poems by blacks.

I have become distressed at the young black people who are coming up now. Too many young black college students are selfish young people with no concern for anyone less fortunate than them and unwilling to give anything back to the black community that made their success possible. I believe that black kids need all of us to participate in their success, so I often invite the black cafeteria workers to come into my class to hear students read or to show off their work.

I became a teacher because it was one of the few careers open to blacks with degrees. It was either social work or teaching for black women. It was even more difficult for black men. At that time black men considered themselves lucky if they could get a position with the post office. But very few black men were able to get jobs teaching in Boston when I graduated from college. My first position right after graduation was at the Alcott School, on West Concord Street in the South End. At the time I started teaching in Boston most black teachers were assigned to a narrow geographic strip from the South End into Roxbury, between Tremont Street and Washington. Those assigned to schools outside that area had a very hard time. I taught at the Alcott School for nine years, until I was assigned to the Hurley, another predominantly black school.

When the schools were desegregated in 1974, black teachers were dispersed throughout the system and I was sent to the Millmore, a predominantly white school. There was a lot of bitterness among the white teachers throughout the system. Some were bitter because their friends had been reassigned to other schools; others were resentful that for the first time they had to work under black principals or alongside black teachers. Most of the white teachers at the Millmore School didn't speak to me or associate with me during the years I taught there.

There have been a lot of changes during the thirty-three years I have been teaching. First, teaching is much more difficult than it was. There is less commitment among teachers who often distance themselves from parents and communities, and there is much more specialization. Years ago teachers taught all students in their own classroom, but there wasn't any Chapter I, there wasn't any special education. These special programs were touted as the solution, but they haven't provided the answer to poor achievement. These programs have brought a lot of money into the school system, they have hired a lot of extra personnel, and they require a lot of administrative time. But the children enrolled in these special programs aren't doing that much better than they were in the regular classrooms.

If we really want to improve education, we need to move it into the larger community, into settings other than the school setting. We need community reading and learning centers where children could go after school, where adults could accompany them to visits to museums and other places of cultural interest. This would alleviate the problem of after-school care and children wouldn't have to go home to an empty house.

We also need to do something about providing better training to teachers who are going to be working in urban areas. If I were in charge of preparing teachers to work in urban settings, first, I would require students to visit several urban school classrooms before actually enrolling in a teacher education program. How can they correctly assess whether they can work or want to work in urban schools if they have never been inside one? I would also screen prospective teachers for their ability to work with urban children. Teaching urban children effectively requires more than good teaching techniques. It requires the ability to solve problems; it requires commitment, psychological strength, and determination. It requires the ability to interact and talk with children, so that you can get across the idea that you are interested in their success and that you are not going to accept anything less than their absolute best in your classroom. Once students began the teacher education program, I would place them in the classroom to apprentice under master teachers, teachers who have a proven track record working with urban black students. I believe that teachers can learn appropriate teaching methods, but I am not sure that they can learn the essential characteristics for teaching in urban schools. Also I wouldn't be afraid to wash out teacher candidates who just didn't demonstrate the necessary characteristics for the difficult work of teaching in urban schools. If we approached training teachers for urban schools differently, we might stop wasting time and money on those who just don't have what it takes to work successfully in urban schools.

LOUISE MASON

I watch while Louise Mason, a willowy, vivacious woman with a dancer's body, leads ten students through a dance routine. "Listen to the music, legs higher, heads high," she calls out as she claps her hands to mark the beat. Occasionally, she demonstrated the dance steps. A few hours later we are seated at her dining room table.

This is my thirty-fourth year of teaching, twenty-nine in Los Angeles and five in Ohio. When I first began teaching in Cleveland, I was totally unprepared. My first assignment was at Central Junior High School at 40th and Central in a section of Cleveland called Hough. Everyone called the area "tough Hough." I will never forget that first year. I remember coming home frustrated day after day. I had never taught black urban students before; I did my student teaching in an all-white school in Xenia, not far from Wilberforce. I wasn't adequately prepared to teach urban black students. Every day for the first month of school I came home crying. I even thought about quitting teaching until one day when I came home and decided I hadn't gone through four years of college, spent a lot of money, only to have students run me out of the profession. There was one other black teacher at the school and we worked together. We were able to turn the entire physical education program around.

I started teaching at Belmont High School near downtown Los Angeles in 1966 and taught there until 1976. After ten years of teaching in the physical education department, I wanted to expand the dance program, but Belmont could not afford to have one teacher devoted entirely to teaching dance. If I wanted to develop a full-scale dance program, I knew I would have to leave Belmont. So, when a position became available in a Valley school which had the facilities that would allow me to build a dance department, I left. After nine years I returned to Belmont. Hopefully, I will retire from the school.

When I relocated to Los Angeles, I knew I wanted to teach high school, and I wanted to teach in a school with a multicultural, multiethnic student background. Belmont attracted me because it had a mixture of various ethnic groups: Latino, Asian, black, and white. Belmont High School is a little United Nations in Los Angeles. The students come from approximately fifty-nine different countries and there are approximately twenty-nine different languages spoken. It was wonderful to see all kinds of students working together as one, and it seemed that everybody was able to get along. Before coming to Los Angeles, I had taught in Cleveland in predominantly black schools. When I first began teaching at Belmont, I was the only black teacher in the physical education department, but that didn't bother me, because in most of my own schooling experiences I was one of a few blacks.

After I left to go teach in the Valley, Belmont School went through a difficult period. Gangs started coming onto the campus, graffiti started appearing on the walls, and the school janitors became lax as far as keeping the campus clean. The school got a bad reputation; it wasn't seen as one of the better schools in the district. Eventually they hired the principal who really turned the school around. It was great to come back to Belmont and be able to work under him. But he was successful, so now he has gone downtown to the central administration. He trains other principals and teachers who work with schools with students from many different ethnic backgrounds.

I am one of the faculty sponsors of the Martin Luther King Club. Our school has a variety of clubs: the Vietnamese Club, the Chinese Cultural Club, the Mexican-American Club. The Martin Luther King Club is made up mostly of black students on campus.

Overall, I haven't been happy with the participation. Even though there aren't many black students at Belmont—about 3 percent—there's enough of them there to have a nice, sizable Martin Luther King Club. Unfortunately, not all of the black students at Belmont participate. When I first began teaching, there were many more black students here. But over the years there moved out of the area, and they are just starting to come back now.

Belmont is really a great place to work. I love the kids. They are respectful, and teachers don't have the constant parent interference and meddling that you have in some of the other areas. Part of the physical education program involves taking students to dance and theater performances. We have gone to the Joffrey, the American Ballet Theater Company, the Alvin Ailey Dance Company, and the Dance Theater of Harlem. The Martin Luther King Club has sponsored trips to the Afro-American Museum in Los Angeles. My purpose is to make students aware of some of the activities that take place outside of the school building. It thrills me to see the students attending a dance or to attend a theater performance or a museum exhibit for the first time.

I never had a black teacher until college. That may seem unbelievable in a city like Philadelphia, but because I attended school outside of my district I didn't encounter any black teachers, all of whom were clustered in predominantly black schools. Until college, all of my teachers, from elementary school through high, were white. In my elementary, junior high, and high schools I was one of only two or three other blacks in the schools. There were three of us black students that all went through school together, to the same schools. At that time I wasn't very aware of color. I enjoyed being with certain people, whether they were white students or whether they were black friends of mine. I remember that I got along with everybody and that I participated in everything.

But looking back now I can see the racism in the schools I attended in the Philadelphia public school system. I remember that most of the black students in high school were being steered to go into the clerical field. The counselor at Germantown High School, who was supposed to be guiding me, told me that I was not college material, that I should go into the clerical field. At the time I knew exactly what I wanted to do. My mind was set on being a physical education teacher. Even though I was only an average student—I did not have all A's—I knew that if I worked for what I wanted, I could do it. Being a physical education teacher was what I wanted, so I just listened to her and then I went on about my business, planned my own college career, and went on from there.

When I was choosing colleges I picked Wilberforce, because being from the North I knew I didn't want to deal with the racism in the South, and I decided to go to the Midwest. But I had a rude awakening. I found a lot a racism right there in southern Ohio. Black people were not allowed to go to various establishments in the area, they were not allowed to buy homes in many towns. Southern Ohio was very racist. So while I was in college I got involved with the NAACP and under the auspices of SCLC (Southern Christian Leadership Conference) I marched and picketed in southern Ohio.

I wanted to go to a "black college" because I had never had any black teachers, and I wanted to learn more about black history. The history that I was taught in Philadelphia was United States history and European history, but there was nothing that dealt with black people other than George Washington Carver, Booker T. Washington, and maybe Mary McLeod Bethune was thrown in there somewhere, but it wasn't covered well enough that I felt that I knew anything about my history. So I made up my mind that I was going to attend a black college to learn about my own history and also to study under black teachers.

The best part about teaching is being able to relate to young people, being able to understand and sympathize with some of the problems that they are having. The physical education class is not as structured as English, math, or science. The kids feel a little closer to a person who can sit down on the floor and do a roll with them. In my class I never ask the students to do something that I am not willing to try myself. I demonstrate everything and I do everything that I expect my students to do. We run together, jog together. I do gymnastic flips with them and I do dance steps with them. I find that doing all these activities together with students makes them more cooperative. Perhaps the students feel that if their old teacher can get out on the gym floor, they can do it too.

I present myself to the students in such a way that they know if they have a problem that they don't want to go to their mother about, if they don't feel they have anyone else to talk to, they can always talk to me and the problem will be held in the strictest confidence. I am the kind of teacher whom students feel comfortable with, the kind of teacher whose students come and tell me their problems. I can't begin to tell you the kinds of problems I have encountered as a teacher: children who have been abused, who are strung out on drugs, or have tried to commit suicide. I have taken in students on a temporary basis until they could be placed in a foster home because their parents threw them out of the house. I have had to get medical care for a student who tried to do an abortion on her own. There have been many situations like this in my teaching career. Helping students deal with these problems is what my teaching job consists of. My job is not just teaching in the physical education program. It is dealing with my students as if they were a part of my extended family.

Integration has been a beginning but we have such a long way to go. Integration allowed us to stay in various hotels, eat at certain restaurants, and spend our money in various establishments. If we judge the success of integration by where we can spend our money, then I would have to say that integration has enabled us to participate in the larger society. But if the measure of integration is whether we are able to participate in the society as producers as well as consumers, then I don't think integration has been as successful, because integration hasn't promoted economic development in the black community nor has it improved the economic well-being of most black people. Too many white people still don't want us to live next door to them, to belong to their clubs. In that sense we aren't further ahead. We still have racism in our society, North, South, East, and West.

As far as black students are concerned, the ghost of racism haunts them in ways that are foreign to me. Even though I grew up in a poor Philadelphia neighborhood, I felt secure and hopeful about my future. Too many of today's black children don't feel safe because they live in neighborhoods where they are surrounded by gangs, drugs, and violence. The state of California has shown that it is willing to spend as much money as it takes to lock them up but almost nothing to educate them properly. Given these conditions, millions of young black people have no reason to be hopeful about their future.

BOBBIE DUVON

*Hair closely cropped, Bobbie Duvon is stylishly dressed in a
dark suit. Several times, our conversation at West End High
School in Hartford, Connecticut, is interrupted by the peal of
bells signaling the beginning and end of classes. Files and
papers cover her desk.*

*Duvon grew up in Dante (pronounced Daint), a coal-
mining community in West Virginia. Her father worked as
an orderly and later as a physician's assistant in the company hospital. Her mother taught in the public schools for
several years but opened her own store when she discovered
it was more profitable. One of three girls, Bobbie attended a
two-room, two-teacher elementary school in Dante. Later
she lived with relatives in Pennsylvania and New Jersey
while attending school. Because there was no high school
for blacks in Dante, she went to Swift Memorial Junior College, a boarding school in Tennessee that included grades
seven through the second year of college. After graduating
from West Virginia State University she taught in Wheeling,
West Virginia.*

I've been teaching in Hartford for thirty-three years and for the
most part I've enjoyed it. I've been at this school twenty-one
years, three years as vice principal. My primary duties are to handle discipline. Every so often something happens that makes me
think that it is time for me to leave teaching. A few days ago I got

very upset with a parent. Two kids were involved in a fight. Whenever kids are involved in a fight, I call the parents and students in.
We have a three-way conversation and we try to work it out. These
same kids had been in a fight last year. We told them if it happened
again they would be out the full ten days. I hate to suspend kids,
because when they're home they're not getting any education. So I
rarely suspend kids. One mother just sat there with her son, while
the father was expounding that his son wouldn't fight. I asked the
father how he knew this. I don't think you can predict what another
person will do; you can only say what you would do under those circumstances. But the father wouldn't hear anything I was saying.
Eventually I told him that if his son was caught fighting again, if he
caused another disruption in school, then he was up for expulsion.
But the conference didn't go as I wanted it to because we never
resolved anything. After that conference I felt as though it must be
time for me to retire. But confrontations with parents are rare. Most
of the problems I have in this school are with the faculty.

When I came here the student population was less than 1 percent minority; now it's 90 percent minority, mostly Hispanic. The
student population has changed quite a bit. Unfortunately our
staff has not. It is still predominately white. I have no problems
with white teachers, or white anybody, but the attitude that too
many of them come here with—and some who have been here a
long time have—is that the kids' parents don't care or that they
don't speak English. All parents care about their kids. They may
not respond the same way that other parents do, but, regardless,
teachers have to treat parents and kids with respect.

We have been trying to get teachers to change their attitudes
toward the kids and to raise their expectations of kids. But when
these teachers see all of these black and Hispanic faces, and the
different kinds of clothes they wear, too many of them have
already decided that the kids aren't capable of learning anything.
The teachers decide that they can't teach the way they did twenty
years ago, because these students would never understand. What
they don't understand is that they could still teach the same
material, but they may have to change the way they present the
material and the attitude they display toward the kids.

These kids can pick up a negative attitude immediately. They can read teachers. Teachers can fool other grown-ups, but they can't fool kids. If you don't like them, the kids can tell it right away. They can tell right away the vibes that are going out. Too many teachers don't treat kids with respect, yet they expect them to respect them; it's really one-sided.

Some of the work we're doing with teachers is beginning to pay off. The teachers are more involved in discipline, but we've had to help them learn how to deal more effectively with the students. Before we implemented that policy, anytime teachers were having a problem with a kid they used to come down to my office and want me to solve it for them. I would ask the teacher what they had done. Had they spoken with the student? Had they called the parent? Usually the teachers wanted me to call the parents, which I refused to do because I wasn't the one having the problem. Or the teacher would claim that the parents wouldn't answer the phone or that they didn't care. Now teachers are encouraged to keep the students after school to try and resolve the problem. And if that fails, teachers are encouraged to call home. When the teachers do call home, they are often surprised at the kind of support they get. Generally, they don't have any more problems with the student after that.

Sometimes just talking with the student makes a difference. We also have tried to get the teachers to understand today's adolescents. We encourage teachers to get students involved in establishing and discussing class rules and the consequences for breaking them, and if students don't like the rules we encourage them to give good reasons for altering the rules.

Another problem we have had to address is how teachers deal with conflicts with students. It isn't wise to argue with a kid in the class because if you embarrass him, back him into a corner in front of his peers, you probably will have a huge confrontation. It's better to talk to the kid after class when he's not in front of his peers. When I taught kids, and even now in my role as vice principal, I never argue with students.

Some days students come to school and they've had a difficult time. Somebody has bumped them in the hall or something else has happened. In that, they are no different from teachers. Teachers walk into school and perhaps that day someone has cut them off on the highway, so they are mad and in a bad mood. We're trying to get teachers to recognize that kids come to school with problems and encourage the teachers to handle the problem within the confines of the classroom. After all, if the teachers can't handle conflict appropriately, how can we expect kids to learn to handle theirs more appropriately?

It's a fact that kids today are much freer with their expressions. When I first started teaching, kids wouldn't dare say the things to adults that they say now. They might be thinking them, as I did when I was young, but they dared not say it. In their outward expressions today's students are different, but I don't think the kids are any different as far as their emotional needs. A lot has changed around the kids, but basically they want the same thing as I did when I was a child, and as the students that I taught thirty years ago. They want discipline, guidance, and someone to care about them and listen to them.

In my role as vice principal I have to mete out punishment for misbehavior, so quite a few kids pass through these doors. One of the things I have learned to do is listen to what kids have to say. Some of the students get into trouble simply because they want attention, and negative attention is often better than none. Often their misbehavior stems from problems that have to do with parents, family, boyfriends, peers, problems that have nothing to do with what happened in the classroom. After we've finished dealing with whatever they were here for, I always ask them if they want to talk about anything else. Almost all of them will start talking about something that's not at all related to school. Mostly, they want someone to talk to, someone who will listen, who will be nonjudgmental.

People who are not in the school system have extremely negative perceptions of schools, the teachers, and the kids. Most of them think that if they walk into schools they are going to see students armed to the teeth with guns, kids constantly fighting and battling, and drugs being dealt right under their nose. If they were to walk into this school they would see that there is order, that there is respect, and that there is some learning going on. I'm not saying we don't have problems, but the perception that people have of kids is based entirely on what they see on the outside. The public does not have a very high regard for school people because they blame us for everything that's happened to the kids. But adults have become estranged from young people, and consequently many aren't getting the guidance they need at home.

The estrangement is magnified when these young people are black and Hispanic and all the teachers are white. In this school there always seems to be some reason why, if a new teacher comes, it's always another white person. The school system says they can't find black and Hispanic teachers. Maybe that is the case. But this school system has a long history of discriminating against black teachers. I know because I came up against the discrimination.

I applied for a job in the late forties when I first came to Hartford one summer. Each year I reapplied, but they didn't have any openings, or if they did they never called me. So each year, I returned to West Virginia to teach. When I relocated to Hartford I was working for the parks department. Every once in a while I substitute taught in a white section of town at the Noah Webster School. I was there as a long-term sub, for two months, because a teacher was out on leave. At the end of June my principal asked me what was I going to do the next academic year. When I told her I didn't know, she told me that I should file an application with the school board. I told her it had been in for quite a while, so she called downtown and told them she wanted me appointed to the school. Of course, we all knew where that application had gone: It went in the wastebasket because of the color of my skin. This was in fifty-three when there weren't many black teachers in the city. I was fortunate that my principal liked me because otherwise I wouldn't have gotten the job.

For twelve years I taught in two schools: Noah Webster, in the northeast, and Kanelli, in the south. Both were all-white schools. Several times during the years I was asked if I wanted to move to a school with more black students. I always refused because I thought that others— non-blacks—should get to know us also. I wanted to dispel all the negative things they believed about black folks.

That's how I got into the school system. In this position I am able to influence more students than I did as a teacher. Each kid that comes here starts anew. Even though I have their records I don't look at them because I want kids to start a new year and have a new day. I want them to believe that whatever their past they can start over again. We can't tell kids that because they did wrong in previous years their future is sealed. What would have happened to us if our parents and teachers had done that?

Sometimes I can't make any headway with the teachers. Even if the teacher isn't doing the job, it is almost impossible to get a teacher fired. It's time-consuming; in order to have a solid case you have to spend all of your time documenting. In the meantime you're falling behind in all of your other work. Sometimes it's not worth the hassle, especially when you know it still might not be enough to terminate a teacher. In the meantime kids are being hurt.

Once I decide I can't get the teachers to change, I start working on the kids. I talk with them to try to get them to see that they are just playing into the teacher's hands, that the teacher wants them out of the classroom because she really doesn't want to teach them. Sometimes I point out the fact that the kids who are doing well in the class are all white and ask them why they think that is so. I tell the kids that there's nothing I can do about a particular teacher but suggest that they go back into the class and learn, that they shouldn't let anyone, including a teacher, keep them from getting what they need later in life. The only reason some black people survived was because they decided that no matter how bad the situation, we were going to make it. Sometimes black people achieved just to spite a white teacher, to show that they could be successful. I try to get the kids to achieve for themselves, but if that doesn't work, I get them to redirect their anger and turn it into revenge, getting even with the teacher by proving them wrong. I've given up trying to change the system and begun working to change one kid at a time.

Not too long ago there were plans to implement a policy that in order to play varsity sports a student had to have a C average. Some of the biggest opposition to this policy came from white teachers, who claimed that sports were the only reason some black kids didn't drop out and stayed in school. Too many of our black athletes have been used and continue being used by high schools and in colleges. They spend four or five years in high schools and the same amount of time in college, and when they come out they still don't know anything. None of these white teachers would allow their sons or daughters to play sports if they were failing their subjects or just barely passing; their kids would be home studying.

MABEL BETTIE MOSS

We talked in mid-August, only a few weeks before the start of school. As we spoke, she pulled materials from brown manila folders stacked up on her coffee table. Casually dressed in dungarees and a T-shirt, Mabel Bettie Moss talked enthusiastically about growing up in Philadelphia. She graduated from Cheney State University in 1961 and has been teaching in Philadelphia since then.

A teacher has to have imagination and enthusiasm, and both have to be renewed. That is why I never teach in the summers. If I have taught all year, and have done it correctly, I don't have anything left to give children during the summer school. Teachers need to have a life if they are going to bring something into the classroom. A lot of teachers I know, especially those who teach summer school, don't have anything else to do, so they teach summer school. It isn't that they need the money; they just don't know what else to do with themselves. As a result too many of them never develop any kind of interests. They aren't interesting to the children because they have nothing to bring them. During the summer I read, travel, take courses that interest me, and engage in conversation. That's how I renew my enthusiasm for classroom teaching. When I work with new teachers, I tell them that continually developing themselves is the best route to becoming good teachers. Only after they understand the importance of self-development are they ready to teach.

Everywhere I look I see things that have real possibilities for my classroom. A teacher always has to be open to the possibilities that lie outside of the prescribed curriculum if they really want to reach their children. If you look around here you will see that I've got all these folders in which I've collected material for my class, material I have cut out from newspapers and magazines. Earlier in the summer I was reading the newspaper and I found something that said, "squashing bugs." In another magazine I saw something else that said, "bugs out and doing a smashing job." Now, I don't have any bugs in my curriculum, but I can fit that right in somewhere. I found something else that said, "chilled them," and I cut it out because I liked the tone. And I happened to come across another phrase that read, "the challenge of a lifetime." I'm not sure exactly how they fit together—yet. They could be an idea for a story.

One of the major complaints that I have about my teacher training, and about teacher education in general, is there is too much emphasis on teaching people how to teach. I believe that the programs should emphasize subject matter more than teaching techniques. I attended Cheyney University in Pennsylvania. There, they emphasized children's literature—*A Snowy Day* and all the books written specifically for children—instead of literature. Instead of learning world literature, African literature, we spent the majority of our time learning children's literature. A teacher can become familiar with children's literature overnight. Children need to learn to love the written word and the spoken word, and teachers can't convey that love to children unless they have that background themselves. Teacher education students should read and read and read and read, and once they have that love of reading and of literature, then, and only then, should they be allowed to teach children. I read Ishmael Reed, I read Nikki Giovanni, I read other black poets, and that's what I teach my children.

Cheyney Teachers College is a school that has a long history of educating black teachers. Originally the school was located in Philadelphia. Then, it was known as The Institute for Colored Youth. In its earliest years it was headed by Fannie Jackson Coppin, a famous black woman who was born a slave and who later graduated from Oberlin College in Ohio. When the school moved out of Philadelphia, it was renamed Cheyney State Normal School, then it became Cheyney State Teachers College, and now it is known as Cheyney University of Pennsylvania.

When I attended Cheyney between 1957 and 1961, the school had too many rules. Students weren't allowed to ride in cars. We could only go home one weekend a month. In fact, after my first year at Cheyney, I left the campus, because it seemed to me that the people who ran the campus didn't trust the students. At least they didn't trust the female students. The boys didn't have many rules at all, but the girls had to sign out, everywhere we went, and we had strict curfews.

We spent most of our time figuring out how to get around the rules. When I first got there, somebody told me to make friends with students on the first floor, so then when I went out I could put my night clothes in their room. Then when I came back, I could sneak around to their room, tap on the window, climb in the window, put on my night clothes, and walk upstairs.

We had to make up our beds before we went to class, and every day someone—the housemother—checked our room. Well, the "before breakfast bed-making" rule didn't make any sense to me, so I didn't obey it. Usually I would get up, go to class, and then at lunchtime I'd go back to the dorm and that's when I would make up my bed. Of course, since I was breaking the rule, the housemother kept writing me up. The straw that broke the camel's back happened around the debate team. I was on the debating team and was supposed to go to Pittsburgh to attend a debating conference. The housemother said I couldn't go because I hadn't been making up my bed. Her excuse was that I would be a poor representative of the school. This seemed so unreasonable to me that I decided to go to see the president of the university, who never saw students, to get permission to go. The president and the dean of students supported the housemother and wouldn't let me participate. I was furious because I had come from a home where my mother always trusted me and let me speak my mind when I disagreed. I was so angry at their arbitrariness that I became a day student and for the next three years I commuted from home.

There were also some professors that were especially dogmatic. In class, one professor said something that was wrong and

I told her that she was wrong. Everyone laughed; mainly they laughed as a nervous reaction because they weren't used to hearing a student disagree with a professor. Later on when it was time for my in-class training, this same professor wanted to place me in south Philly in the Smith School. I argued that the placement didn't make sense since I lived in north Philly. The night before I was supposed to go, another professor called me up and told me that she was going to reassign me to north Philadelphia. When I graduated the professor disclosed that the other woman had pulled the strings to get me to go to south Philly so that she could be in charge of me and flunk me because I had contradicted her in class. Although I have a certain fondness for Cheney, I felt there was quite a bit of pettiness to contend with, and I felt that insofar as actually teaching us enough subject matter, the curriculum was deficient. But, for the most part, the teachers were very knowledgeable and some of them were quite exceptional.

Cheyney definitely influenced my views about teaching. The influence of educators like Fannie Jackson Coppin, who had devoted their lives to educating black students permeated the place. As a student at Cheyney I had the sense that I was part of a long tradition with a definite mission of teaching black children. The professors preached the message that we had a responsibility to black children. As a student there were times when I thought they overemphasized the message. They really stressed the fact that somebody had helped us get where we were and that we had a responsibility to give something back to the community, to make a contribution to the black community. Since most of us were preparing to be teachers, we were expected to teach black children well. That was a real strong and consistent message. They also taught us that black people should support each other and that for the sake of the community we were bound to be the best at whatever we chose to do. It wasn't until much later when I began teaching and saw how often black children weren't being taught well that I understood the significance of the message.

I have been teaching in this community—in the same school—since 1961, and I can really see the negative effect that drugs have had on the community. The way things are going, it's only going to get worse. In the late eighties, we had a drug house right across from our school, right across from the schoolyard. With the grip that crack cocaine has on our community a lot of the mothers are simply unable to cope. Crack cocaine is so cheap and it grabs them so fast. In this community, more and more grandmothers are raising their grandchildren, and although many of them do a fantastic job others are simply too worn out to raise another generation. One little girl in my class last year is being raised by her grandmother, a sickly woman, who has six children in her home under twelve from three different daughters, all victims of crack cocaine.

In the past, if I couldn't get the parents to cooperate with me, I could generally call grandmothers for support. If a child wasn't doing well, if their mother wasn't being responsive to my calls, I would call the grandmother and say, "You know that girl of yours, she isn't doing what she's supposed to do." I used to do that all the time. Often the daughters would get upset with me and ask me why I had called their mothers. But now that the extended family and community—the infrastructure—is slowly disappearing, that strategy simply doesn't work anymore. The neighborhood is under siege, and the children have to be able to walk through a minefield if they are to survive.

In this neighborhood the children either do well or they do poorly. There doesn't seem to be anything in the middle. When I say they do well, I don't mean that they all attend college. Some do become doctors and lawyers. Others graduate from high school, get responsible jobs, and become fine people. But too many become addicted to drugs, get murdered, or land up in jail. That's the way of the neighborhood. The children have to get out of the neighborhood for a while to do better. Once they've done better they can come back. But they have to go away to school or go away to the army or just go away, because the neighborhood just eats them alive.

One of the most troubling trends cropping up among the children is their preoccupation with "light skin–dark skin, good hair and bad hair." Many of the things that we seemed to have accomplished in the sixties—things that I thought were permanent changes—have been coming back, slowly, and now they seem to be stronger than ever. Seeing the children's obsession with color has made me realize that it wasn't a permanent change. Too many of the children just adore the light-skinned children. And the girls just fawn over boys who have light skin. They want to play with their hair. They look up to children who are dressed in the latest styles. It doesn't matter if the children don't have any character.

In class I find myself constantly bringing up these issues. Sometimes they look at me like I don't know what I am talking about, and I tell them, "I know you're looking at me, and I know you're saying to yourself, 'Miss Moss is old. Miss Moss doesn't know what she is talking about.' But I am discussing these issues because I have to, because I can't ignore things that are harmful to us and our community." So I keep addressing these issues over and over again because this obsession with consumerism, material goods, and physical beauty promotes false values.

Instead of buying into these false values, I want my students to develop more positive values, to establish solidarity with each other, not to fight, argue, and bicker with each other all of the time. They are able to stick together, but it's generally around unimportant issues. Occasionally they'll decide among themselves on a color to wear, and then they'll all show up wearing that color. It is amazing. I tell them that if they can stick together for something as unimportant as fashion, then they ought to be able to stick together over more important issues. I have them practice supporting each other when their friends tease them for learning. We work on that in class so they won't be ashamed of learning or using their minds, so they can stand up to the children who make fun for learning, for doing schoolwork.

I lived in the neighborhood where I teach for the first sixteen years, but then it became too much. While I enjoyed the close relationships I had with the community, I felt like I was never off duty. Finally, I moved because I knew that I needed to be emotionally healthy if I was going to be able to continue teaching. Even though I enjoy the peace of mind and quiet, I can't help thinking about the problems in the neighborhood.

I don't consider myself a "touchy-feely" person. Up until three or four years ago I would never hug the children, had them hold onto me, or hang on me, but now I do it because I have discovered just how important it is for the children to have someone embrace them emotionally and physically. The children need the closeness. Now when they come up and hold onto me, and it will be six of them at a time, I just rub their backs and hug them.

In all of my years of teaching I have yet to meet a child that couldn't learn. There are many reasons that children don't learn in school. Some of them don't want to. Some of them don't know why they should learn school material. For some, learning isn't made very attractive. And in so many instances school is just so boring and unrelated to their everyday lives. Occasionally, when I have gone into other teachers' rooms and seen what is going on, I have realized how awful it would be to have to be a student in that classroom. Too many teachers make learning so boring. If you want to make learning attractive, you have to constantly bring things from the outside world into the classroom. You have to keep surrounding children with new ideas until something strikes them and catches their attention. I consider myself a teacher, but I'm also a learner. To be a teacher, you also have to be a learner.

Having taught in the same school for as long as I have is an enormous advantage because I taught their mothers, their fathers, their uncles, their aunts, cousins, and their neighbors. So the children know about me before they even get to school. My involvement with parents has often gone beyond our mutual interest in their children. Over the years I have encouraged a lot of women to return to school to earn their GED. When parents return to school to earn their GED or when they enroll in college, the children seem to benefit. Over the years I have had students whose mothers have attended community college. It is remarkable to see the difference in their children's classroom performance. Parents tell me that once they enroll in college, they often spend time sitting down and doing their homework together with their children. When parents interact with their children over homework, the message they send is much greater than the message they send by simply telling children schoolwork is important. But recently the state has made it harder and harder for people to go to school.

This year I am teaching sixth-graders. Although I have always taught intermediate grades—I taught fourth grade and fifth grade the longest—I enjoy sixth grade most because the children are beginning to develop into people. It's fascinating to watch and be a part of that process. One of the problems in teaching the upper grades is the poor preparation that some of the children get in the lower grades. Too many of the lower grade teachers in my school don't adequately prepare the students for the kind of work they will be required to do in the upper elementary grades. The teachers don't stretch the children's minds, and it is very noticeable when they come to me. The children are used to sitting and writing in the workbooks. So all they want to do in my class is open up a workbook and do exercises. In the middle grades, I want them to talk, ask questions, and express themselves. In the lower grades they never seem to discuss anything significant. They just have these little rote drills. The only time students get to talk is when they are answering the teacher. Students should be the ones doing the talking. In my class, I want the children to do the talking because only then are they doing the learning.

My students know that they have to learn something every day, even if it's just a little bit. I try to impress upon them that learning is part of their responsibility to themselves, their families, and their community. The first question I ask them every day is why they are in class. Every day they answer, "We're here to learn something." Once they answer that, we go on to the day's activities. At the end of every day we talk about what we learned. We also discuss what they didn't learn. The children know that even though I may have taught something one day if any one of them didn't learn it I am going to teach it again until everybody learns it. So if they didn't learn it today, they don't get discouraged. They also know that if they don't know something or didn't learn something that it's not their fault.

If a child says, "Ms. Moss, I can't read," I acknowledge what they have said. But I never say, "Now, what's the matter with you, boy?" or anything that suggests impatience on my part. When the children tell me they can't do something, I never tell them, "There's no such word as can't." Instead I will say, "I know you can't do it now, but we'll work together and soon you will be able to do it on your own." Because there is a can't. There's a whole lot of reasons they can't do something. But I want them to just keep persevering until they can. I have a lot of patience. The only thing children can do to upset me is deliberately keep the other children from learning.

Teaching is an art; that's why it's hard to evaluate. That's why it is foolish to depend only on test scores to evaluate a teacher's performance or determine what is going on in a classroom. Of course, I keep my test scores up, because then the principal and supervisors can't use that against me. I'm almost at the end of my career, and although I enjoy teaching I am glad that I will be getting out of the school system soon. Teachers don't get any support at all from the principal, the district superintendent, or the central administration, and it is becoming more physically dangerous. In the past I never feared for my physical safety, but I've started to be fearful now, not of the children in my school but of people who prey on the neighborhood. Several years ago a man came into the school with a gun. He made all the women get down on the floor and held the gun to their heads and he took their pocketbooks. Incidents like that have made me uneasy and fearful. One day when I was walking up the street a teenager was following me very closely. All of a sudden I stopped and turned around very quickly. He sensed my fear and said, "I wasn't gonna take your bag, Miss." Then he recognized me and said, "Ms. Moss." When he called my name I remembered him as a student who had been in my class.

There's also the paperwork, so much unnecessary paperwork. I am constantly filling out reports and forms, and then they take them and file them in the office. Nobody ever looks at them, but I spend so much time on paperwork. There's even more paperwork from the Board of Education. All this paperwork just takes up valuable time that I could spend preparing for my classes.

Most teachers don't appreciate black children and their strengths. Black kids are creative, inquisitive, and bright. That's the best word to describe them. Every year my students seem to get better and better, but working in the system has become almost impossible.

Part III

THE NOVICES

LEONARD COLLINS

Leonard Collins was raised in Los Angeles and in Riverside, California. Twenty-three years old, he is zealous, passionate, and forthright. A second-year teacher, he works in San Bernadino County. Three Saturdays a month he volunteers at Imani School, an Afrocentric supplementary school. He is an active member of the All African Peoples Revolutionary Party. The day after we talked, he was flying to the East Coast to visit a graduate program in African-American studies.

Although I am concerned with all students, African students—by that I mean black students—are my primary focus. Some people disagree with my use of the word African to describe black people, but I think that by calling all of us African, it forces us to recognize that we all come from the same area of land. I want black students to learn about themselves from a black perspective. Usually we learn about ourselves from a deficit point of view. We learn that we were slaves, that we picked cotton, that we didn't contribute anything to the world. Those were my experiences in school. I grew up in all-white neighborhoods and attended predominantly white schools from first through fifth grade. I wanted to be like the white kids because they had all the things that I didn't have. My materialistic attitude consumed me.

When I was in school, I never felt good about who I was and, although I hate to admit it, I didn't like the fact that I was black. I never felt positively about the next black person. I was always angry and frustrated during my school years but I didn't know why. I was frustrated by the way my teachers interacted with me. They didn't expect me to be a successful student. It wasn't anything that they said specifically. It was just the way they approached me. As I got older I began learning that black people had suffered, that we had been oppressed although I didn't think of it in exactly those terms. When I got to high school I began to understand more about oppression and began learning phrases like "institutional racism." But I didn't believe I could do anything about it. When I got to college I met a person who helped me understand my frustration, taught me about being African, and how to focus my anger toward something positive. I don't want to see other black kids going through what I experienced.

I teach third grade. My class is about one-third black, one-third white, the others include a few Asians. Schools are meant to socialize kids into everything that I don't agree with. That's one of the contradictions that I have to deal with in my teaching. That forces me to be a reactionary teacher. I spend all of my time countering the prescribed curriculum, saying to kids, "Let's look at this critically. Let's look at this from a different perspective." For example, in social studies, the textbooks describe how Christopher Columbus discovered America or how the Pilgrims or the settlers came over to the United States. Although the textbook might mention that the settlers learned a lot of things from the Indians, it doesn't discuss how the settlers exploited the Indians for their land. They don't discuss the disease and pestilence that they brought over from Europe. So I delve into that. I have students examine that same historial event but from a different perspective. I don't tell the students that white people are bad or that Europeans are bad people. I simply present an alternate perspective and let the students come to their own conclusions.

I want kids to examine their world critically, to question everything. As kids get older they automatically accept the American ideology. But I don't want kids to just be the future; I want them to change the future. So far, I haven't had any negative repercussions from the parents. Some of them have questioned why I don't say the Pledge of Allegiance in the classroom. I told them we have a Jehovah's Witness in the classroom and I want to respect all of the students' backgrounds. That's how I handled it. The principal doesn't know what I am doing in my classroom. I shut my door and do what I want.

Teachers have a tendency to promote patriotism. They glorify European contributions, everything European. Teachers don't denigrate the contributions of people, they just skip over them. They never address the perspectives of people of color. I put Africans within the context of everything that I teach. I do this with other cultures as well. For example, when I taught about the transcontinental railroad, I showed my class how Asians were exploited, how they were denigrated during this whole process. I try to show what role each group has played throughout history. I do this in anything that I teach but especially in social studies. By simply presenting the perspectives of people of color, I believe I am making a contribution.

Teaching at Imani School is totally different than in public school. At Imani we place Africa at the focal point. In an African-centered school, everything starts in Africa, then branches out. If we talk about math, we highlight the role that Africans played in developing mathematics. When we read stories, we read about the African experience. I don't want to glorify Africa unnecessarily, but I think it's important for students to know how Africans were involved in everything we are studying. Instead of being on the outside looking in, we are central players. At Imani I can be a proactive teacher rather than a reactionary teacher, as in public school.

Personally, I believe that socialism would be a better system for organizing society. I don't promote this idea to my kids because third-graders aren't old enough understand it. However, I do talk about the ills of capitalism, but I don't use those words. We discuss why it's wrong to go to school just to make a lot of money or why it's wrong to sell drugs to make money. Every one of them will be approached about drugs before they reach high school. I try to expose the problems with capitalism rather than promote some other economic system.

I try to counter individualism. For example, if one kid gets into trouble in my class, then the whole class pays for it. My goal is to get them to be responsible for each other rather than being concerned only with themselves individually. Sometimes this strategy backfires, but they do monitor each other's behavior and they think twice before they misbehave because they don't want a negative reaction from their peers.

I haven't been able to use that strategy when it comes to

grades, because I am bound to give grades. The only time I give grades is on report cards. For each assignment I tell students the number of answers they got right and wrong. They always know how they performed. Even though I am promoting competition by giving grades, I award them because otherwise I might compromise their doing well. I don't want to say, "We don't know who's doing well and who's not doing well." If they aren't doing well, they are going to know it. I want the best out of them because I have high expectations for all of my students. When it comes to their schoolwork, I am quite hard on students. I expect their writing to be correct. I expect it to be thought-provoking. I want them to take their time to do their best work.

We desegregated but we never integrated. Integration never happened. Most black folks live among each other. When black folks get money, they go and live among white folks because white folks are the ones with the money. If we were truly integrated, when we went for a job, we would have the same chance of getting that job. If we were truly integrated, when we applied to go to college, we would have the same chance of getting in. If we were truly integrated the education we receive in elementary school would be comparable to that of whites. Integration will never happen under capitalism, because people who espouse it and benefit by it don't want to give up control of the resources. Whites don't want to give up control. I don't believe in integration because in an integrated society our issues are not central.

I want my African students to learn to love themselves and I want them to learn to love each other. We don't understand each other because we don't know ourselves. This lack of knowledge is the cause of most of the problems among black people. Much of the conflict we see in community starts in school because we don't learn about ourselves or see ourselves in the curriculum.

The only thing I can do is teach my kids to question authority, question what the teacher says, not to be submissive. I want them to be critical but to be smart about what they do. But if they are too cautious, they will fall into to the same trap as people who were in the movement in the sixties. Once they got more responsibility, got their good jobs, their families, and their houses, they stopped being critical of the world.

Black people don't go into teaching because they have had negative experiences in school. They also don't go into teaching because they are materialistic. Teachers don't get paid enough. That's the overwhelming sentiment among young black students. If you ask them, "Why don't you go into teaching?" they say, "Teachers don't get paid enough." You hear that time and time again. I didn't decide to become a teacher until my junior year in college. At first I was a business major. I wanted to be a big business executive and make a lot of money. But when I started learning about capitalism, I felt as if I would be contributing to the exploitation of black people. My current salary is eight times what I was making as a college student. It's darn good money. But money's not the reason why I teach. All I need is someplace to live and some means of transportation. I don't live in this world to become rich, I want to live in this world to serve humanity.

ASHALLAH WILLIAMS

Although she looks like a teenager, Ashallah Williams is twenty-seven. Animated and charismatic, she punctuates her staccato speech with her hands. She is casually dressed in blue jeans and a sweater. Two gold hoops dangle from her pierced ears and her close-cropped natural hairstyle is encircled by a colorful African print scarf.

Ashallah Williams was born in New York and attended public school in the city. For several years she lived with her grandparents in Virginia and attended public school there. She has been teaching fifth grade in Baltimore, Maryland, for five years.

Almost all of my students are poor and black. They come from single-parent households and live in housing projects. When I see them sitting in my classroom, they remind me of myself. I was the child of an unmarried mother, who was only sixteen when I was born. A year later, at seventeen, she had my brother. Raising us as a single parent in a housing project was a real struggle for my mother. I could easily have been destroyed by my family's circumstances, but I was fortunate to have had people outside of my immediate family who took an interest in me. Some of these people were from my neighborhood, some were from my church, but several of those who reached out to me were teachers. These people were like extended family members and their concern and care enabled me to navigate the treacherous waters of my childhood.

As a young child I wanted to be a teacher, but whenever I said that was my goal, people discouraged me. The teachers at the Bronx High School of Science in New York pushed me into what they thought would be lucrative careers like medicine, engineering, and computer science. They discouraged me by telling me about the low salaries and the lack of prestige. They believed that a young black girl who was good in science and math shouldn't waste her time teaching.

When I work with the children in my classroom, I try to remember myself at that age, what the obstacles were and what my teachers and other adults did that helped me believe that I could overcome the odds, persist, and become successful. The adults who were most helpful in my life were those who took the time to get to know me, my interests, strengths, weaknesses, likes, and dislikes.

I've developed a systematic process of getting to know each of my students. As soon as I get my class list I begin to develop a portfolio for each student. During the summer I visit students' homes and I conduct interviews with the students and with their parents. I ask parents what goals they have for their children, what they think their children should learn in school, and what they believe their children's strengths and weaknesses are. I ask parents about their interests and special skills. Parents have a lot of talents and skills that are useful in the classroom. When I am planning a classroom unit I look at the interests and skills parents have listed and invite parents into the classroom to demonstrate something or participate in one or more classroom activities. My purpose is to develop partnerships with parents so that I can be more responsive to their children's learning, social, and emotional needs.

Students fill out interest, activity, and attitude inventories. Sometimes I ask students to take me on a walk around their neighborhood. All of this information goes into my file. My purpose is to get as much information as I can about each child's interests, likes, and dislikes and use this in my teaching. For instance, during the interviews, I ask each child what topics interest them, what topics they would like to know more about.

My curriculum is eclectic. I am not an ideologue and I refuse to be held hostage to any one view of curriculum—a basic skills approach as opposed to the discovery method. I am interested in what works with my students in my classroom. Sometimes students are working on topics that I have decided upon. At other times they are working on topics of their own choosing. Throughout the year students study and research the topics they have expressed an interest in. If several students have the same interests, they can choose to work together on the same topic. Otherwise each one works on their own. Students are encouraged to become experts on their chosen topic. Periodically they share what they have learned with the rest of the class. Some students work for an entire year on one topic; other students work on several topics during the school year. In this process students learn how to find information about a topic, they learn the vocabulary words associated with the topic, and they end up reading texts that are much more difficult than school texts.

When we study subjects that aren't familiar to my students, I make sure that I connect what we're learning in the classroom to students' lives. Some of the ways that I accomplish this is by taking field trips, by inviting parents and community people into the classroom, by using videos and audiotapes and computer applications. Whenever I teach a lesson I try to have as many ways of presenting the material as possible. I use visuals and three-dimensional objects. I organize hands-on activities. I use drama, song, rap music, and anything else that I think will keep my students interested in what we're learning.

In fifth grade, our science curriculum deals with the human body—the various systems of the human body. Students learn how to take blood pressure readings and interpret them. They use thermometers to take their temperatures and learn how to read them when we learned about basal temperatures. We learn about various diseases, both the accepted medical terms and the terms that are widely used in their communities. It isn't uncommon to hear the expression "yellow jaundice" used by black adults. In many black communities diabetes is referred to as "sugar." Older black people will say, "I have sugar." We talk about why people might use that term instead of the medical term. Some of my students interviewed older relatives who actually had some of the diseases we were studying.

When we studied nutrition students developed different kinds of diets: a low-fat diet, a salt-free diet, one appropriate for someone who had diabetes. We would compare the various diets. On several occasions we prepared some of the meals in the classroom.

Preparing a meal requires students to employ a lot of skills. Usually the menu lists the ingredients required to prepare enough servings for four to six people. In order to adapt the menu for twenty-four diners, students have to use mathematics. They also will have to employ mathematics to do some comparison shopping, to figure out how to stay within our allotted budget. After some of the meals, students have developed and conducted a taste survey with the class and prepared charts and graphs to illustrate findings. In this way, a simple activity like cooking a meal can become a lesson in nutrition, mathematics, and language arts.

I am concerned about my students being proficient in the basic skills of reading, writing, and mathematics. As an open-minded educator, which I consider myself to be, I am not supposed to be overly concerned with basic skills. That's taboo among the more progressive teachers. But many of these progressive white teachers aren't aware that it is one thing for upper middle-class students not to be proficient in basic skills, but it's quite another thing for poor black kids not to be. If the white middle-class students don't know grammar, it is likely to be overlooked, but if poor black students make grammatical mistakes, more than likely it will be seen as a language deficiency or lack of native intelligence. Another reason I don't overlook basic skills is that for some of my parents competence in basic skills is one of the few visible signs that their children are learning the school curriculum. I don't believe that basic skills should be an end in themselves; they need to be learned in the service of something else. Whenever possible I try to embed the basic skills of mathematics and reading and writing into larger activities. But sometimes that's impossible. One of the techniques I use is to make the children responsible for making sure that everyone in the class knows some specific material, like the times tables. They don't let up until everyone in the class knows whatever they are supposed to know. You will see children drilling and reviewing with their classmates on the way to and from school, on the playground, and everywhere else they have a few minutes.

I also use rhythm, rhyme, and rap to teach the children. When we were studying the skeletal system I taught the children the song, "Them bones, them bones, them dry bones." The students learned all of the Latin names for the bones and inserted them into the song. They choreographed an entire routine around that song and every student in the class knew the Latin name of every bone. Whenever anyone came into the class, they wanted to perform the song.

I came to teaching in a roundabout way. After high school I was recruited by several Ivy League schools. I chose Princeton because it wasn't far from New York City. Although I wanted to be a teacher, by the time I got to college I had been convinced that teaching was an undesirable career. So I was a pre-med major and I minored in anthropology. Princeton, especially pre-med, was so competitive that when I graduated I felt isolated, undervalued, and my self-confidence had eroded. I decided to pursue a master's degree in biology at an historically black school before applying to medical school. I applied and was accepted to Hampton. It was a decision that saved me academically and spiritually.

At Hampton the faculty expected me to work hard and to be able to achieve and they never doubted my intellectual competence. At Princeton I always felt I had to prove myself to faculty and to the white students, whom I suspected thought black students were intellectually inferior. Not having to deal with other people's perceptions of my intellectual ability freed me up to concentrate on my academic work. While I was earning my master's degree, one of my professors, a Ghanaian man, convinced me that I should become a teacher. He told me about a program at Hampton that would prepare me to teach in middle school. I already knew how important black teachers were for black students because, even though I only had four black teachers throughout my elementary and secondary school years, those black teachers were the most influential teachers in my educational career. My black teachers were more than role models. The way they interacted with me was familiar. It was as if they were aunts, older sisters, uncles, or a grandmother. It was easier for me to read them, to understand their intentions, and they, mine. So when I learned about the program I enrolled.

Hampton prepared me very well. The courses in biology were rigorous; the methods courses, informative, and I was fortunate enough to be a student teacher in the classroom of a Virginia Teacher of the Year. The most important part of my experience at Hampton was that my professors were always available to help me out in my first years of teaching. Having someone to talk to helped me make it through my early years of teaching.

As much as I enjoy teaching, I don't think I will retire from the profession. Unlike people from previous generations, people from mine don't expect to work at the same career for their entire working lives. For me teaching is one of the first of many careers.